BRAIN *and* LEARNING
Directions in Early Childhood Education

BRAIN *and* LEARNING
Directions in Early Childhood Education

Marlin Languis
The Ohio State University

Tobie Sanders
The Ohio State University

Steven Tipps
University of Virginia

A 1979-80 *Comprehensive* Membership Benefit

National Association for the Education of Young Children
Washington, DC

Photos: Betty C. Ford, *cover*
Jo Leggett, *p. 4*
Ellen Levine Ebert, *p. 18*
Mary K. Gallagher, *p. 23*
Barbara Young, *p. 26*
Elaine Wickens, *p. 31*
Sally Gale, *p. 34*
Michael D. Sullivan, *p. 40*
Elaine M. Ward, *p. 46*
Paul S. Conklin, *p. 51*

Cover design: Caroline Taylor

Copyright © 1980. All rights reserved.
Second printing, December 1980.
National Association for the Education of Young Children
1834 Connecticut Ave., N.W.
Washington, DC 20009

Library of Congress Catalog Card Number: 80-81273
ISBN Catalog Number: 0-912674-72-5
NAEYC #111

Printed in the United States of America

Table of Contents

Preface vii

I. **A Theoretical Perspective** 1–16
   1. New Threads on the Loom 3
   2. Brain Functioning: An Approach to the
      Study of Learning 5
      The Brain
      Brain Models
      Suggested Readings

II. **Brain Functioning: The Study of
    Learning Processes** 17–43
   3. Individuals and Language Development 19
      Motoric Development of Meaning
      Sustaining Independent Speech
      Early Conceptions of Sound and Print Representation
      Suggested Readings
   4. Individuals and Development 27
      Life-Span Development
      Sensitive Periods
      Neurological Development
      Suggested Readings
   5. Individuals, Environment, and Experience 35
      Modeling Revised
      Environmental Messages
      Imagery
      Learning Styles and Exceptionality
      Suggested Readings

III. **Mobilizing for the Future** 45–53
   6. Mobilizing for Individuals 47
      Policy Implications
      Program Implications

References 55
Glossary of Terms 63
Index 67
Selected NAEYC Publications 71

Preface

This book suggests future directions for early childhood education emerging from research and theory in the neurosciences and related disciplines. Professional teachers have always been fascinated and puzzled about how children learn. Teachers and parents deal daily with the brain functioning of young children in the learning contexts of the home and classroom. Brain research provides support for some of the important values of early childhood education, but emerging insights into the working brain raise serious challenges to other aspects of existing educational programs and practices. The initiative and involvement of educators will influence the development of brain research and its implications for both children and adults. This book reflects the interests of teachers and parents in educational settings. It also focuses on leadership personnel involved with policy, planning, and preparation of early childhood education personnel and programs.

The book is organized into three parts. Part I examines theory and evidence for three mutually reinforcing models of how the brain works: an evolutionary model suggesting learning implications of the interaction of parts of the brain; the hemispheric brain model indicating the importance of lateralization and communication between the two halves of the brain, each with a distinctive way of dealing with learning experiences; and a program of the brain models that suggests how learning experiences may result in changes in brain organization and in expectancy.

Part II relates brain functioning theories to the learning process, beginning with three areas of children's language development: the motoric basis for the development of meaning, implications of extended child monologues, and the importance of early conceptions of sound and print for language learning. The next section focuses on the brain's role in individual human development. The third section deals with a generative learning model perspective toward environmental influences on the young child that views the child as an active force who constructs experience through interacting with the environment.

Part III provides a set of recommendations for professional activity to mobilize effective long-term efforts in making futuristic directions in the brain and learning present realities.

Jan McCarthy, NAEYC President 1978–1980, initiated this manuscript for the NAEYC Long-Range Planning Committee whose members reviewed the original draft of this book and recommended its publication.

A note of gratitude is expressed to a number of people for helpful criticism and discussion of the manuscript during its development. For anatomy, brain functioning, and learning theory components: colleagues Rosemarie H. Kraft, University of California at Davis, Merlin C. Wittrock, UCLA, Beth Wismar, The Ohio State University; for suggestions regarding early childhood and human development components: C. Ray Williams, Charles Wolfgang, and Roy Tamashiro, The Ohio State University, and Carl Glickman, University of Georgia.

Our thanks also go to the many outstanding graduate students who have made teaching truly an opportunity to learn as well as a number of people who contributed significantly to manuscript preparation in typing and editorial roles: Becky Rickard, Carolyn Wycuff, Karen Kitts, and Charlotte Phillips at The Ohio State University, and Jan Brown and her staff at NAEYC.

Marlin Languis
Tobie Sanders
Steven Tipps
March 1980

I
A Theoretical Perspective

1
New Threads on the Loom

It is not upon thee to finish the work
Neither art thou free to abstain from it.
—*The Talmud*

The fabric of early childhood education will not be finished in the next 20 years, but recent findings, especially on brain functioning, bring new insights to child development and education. Classical themes of development—sequence, continuity, interrelatedness, and individuality—provide the loom. New knowledge from recent research and theory provides new threads to be woven into the pattern.

Brain functioning research provides one clear source of new information. Brain function is well established as a major area in the scientific research community with definite branches of investigation in hemispheric lateralization, neurological development, cognitive processes, and neurochemistry. Educational literature documents a growing recognition of the educational importance of this area. *Education and the Brain* (Chall and Mirsky 1978), the 77th yearbook of the National Society for the Study of Education, ushered in a new era of interdisciplinary research and application with 11 chapters dealing with the educational implications of neurological findings.

In the book, models of the brain are examined in relation to language, human development, and the interaction between environment and experience. Such an examination suggests—

- fresh and innovative perspectives on traditional concerns of educators;
- a growing set of provocative questions about the learning process;
- expanded empirical and theoretical bases for understanding and influencing learning behaviors; and
- the hint of new directions for early childhood education research and theory, teacher education, programs, and practices in the decades ahead.

A final section explores new directions. Research efforts provide raw fiber for new threads. The spinning process requires knowledge of research and theoretical bases and painstaking transformation into realistic, well-founded practices. We hope to facilitate this process.

2
Brain Functioning: An Approach to the Study of Learning

Brain functioning, an integral part of a new concept of cognition, recognizes both the affective and psychomotor dimensions of learning. Many findings from neurological research support a systems view of the learning process. For example, emotion relates to qualitative differences in cognitive outcomes due to direct interaction between the autonomic part of the brain and the rest of the central nervous system (Buck 1976). The systems view adds a psychophysiological perspective to the familiar whole-child approach in early childhood education.

The systems view supported by brain models is not a simple input-to-output system. New approaches to cognition concentrate on how children and adults create meaning from experience. White and Siegel (1976) defined cognition as getting unconfused.

> . . . to learn is to organize, to extract recurrent regularity from the stimulus flux, to locate information in a "noisy field," to find distinctive features, to reduce uncertainty. (p. 429)

Drawing from brain research, Wittrock (1977, 1978a, 1978b) developed the theme of generative learning. The different meanings individuals generate from similar experiences seem to parallel the differences in strategies available to the human brain. According to Young (1978), extracting information and creating meaning result in programs of the brain. Such programs influence how humans think, communicate, value, feel, help, love, and play.

The Brain

The brain, a pinkish gray mass of nerve cells, weighs about three pounds and is about the size of two fists held together. The brain has

---

Understanding the integrated brain provides a foundation for understanding all aspects of human behavior, including learning and emotions.

a bilateral organization. Paired structures, the left and right brain hemispheres, comprise the cerebral cortex. This organizational feature extends downward into the limbic structures of the midbrain. In addition, sensory and motor pathways cross within the body. The right side of the body feeds sensory information to the left side of the brain and vice versa. Output through motor pathways is similarly crossed. While the brain/body pathways are not exclusively contralateral or crossed in organization, those pathways are considerably stronger than ipsilateral or uncrossed paths.

The nearly identical hemispheres of the brain form the cortex that includes a thin multilayered sheet of cells covering the outside of the brain. Under this grayish outer cover, millions of whitish nerves (axons) connect various areas on the surface of the cortex and connect the cortex with structures deeper in the brain. Other axons connect the brain with the rest of the body through the cranial nerves and spinal cord. Afferent nerves bring messages from the environment inward to the brain via the senses. Efferent nerves carry messages outward from the brain. Along the way nerves have junctions with very small gaps (synapses) where messages can be stopped or sent along depending on the nature and amount of brain transmitter chemicals released into these gaps. Nerves also have branching structures at the end (dendrites) so that a signal from one axon can be transmitted to thousands of other nerves. In addition to the networks of nerves, the brain communicates and interacts with the body and structures within the brain through hormones released by various body organs into the blood. Understanding how the complex communication network functions to connect the brain and body is important in relating the brain to learning.

The midbrain, including the limbic system, consists of a complex of tiny organs, including the thalamus, hypothalamus, hippocampus, olfactory bulb, and amygdala. These organs process information and regulate internal body states and functions through hormones released into the bloodstream and through nerve connections both higher and lower in the nervous system.

The bottom part of the brain is the brain stem, a slender stalk connecting the spinal cord to the limbic system and the cortex. Within the brain stem are groups of cell clusters (nuclei) that form the reticular activating system (RAS). The RAS plays a crucial role in determining environmental stimuli that arouse an individual, focus attention, and result in interaction and experience. Some incoming sensory signals pass through the RAS to higher brain centers, but others are stopped. This is called a gating function. Recent RAS work suggests a complex reciprocal interaction between the RAS and higher cortical areas—perhaps a kind of feedback loop between the planning function of the frontal lobes of the brain and the RAS.

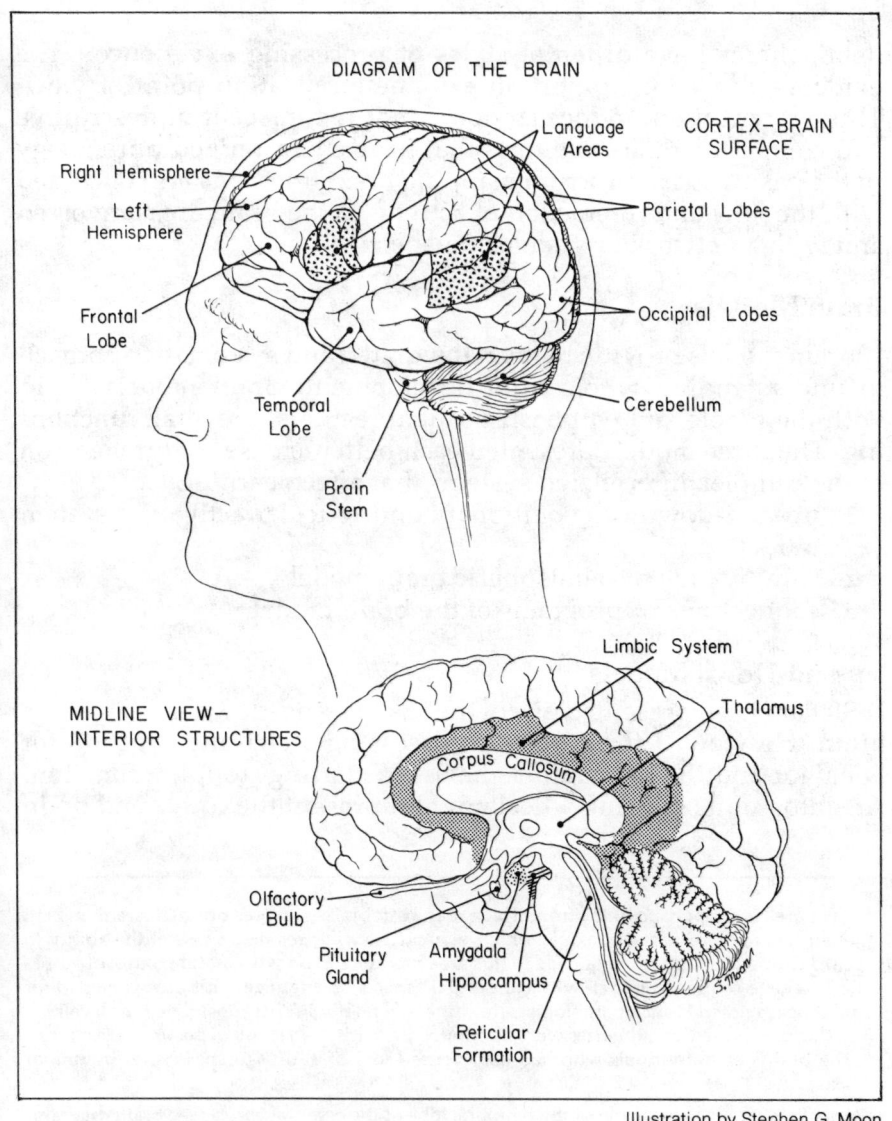

Illustration by Stephen G. Moon

The cerebellum is at the back of the brain, nestled under the cortical hemisphere and attached to the brain stem. The cerebellum is responsible for coordination of basic life processes, muscle coordination, and motor actions of the body.

Evidence has been accumulated over many years that some functions are associated more clearly with somewhat localized areas in the brain than with other areas. For example, Broca's and Wernicke's areas are associated with language functions, and the two cerebral hemispheres have different styles of processing experience.[1] The evidence does not support an extreme localization point of view. Thus, recent work in localization is not reminiscent of descriptive and compartmentalized efforts that have characterized phrenology in the past. Today, efforts in mapping brain functions are concerned with the flow and interaction of activity in the brain areas involved and with a network or systems perspective.

Brain Models

Brain models provide both an integrated and systematic approach to understanding whole-child development. Brain models begin with the whole and emphasize salient features of overall functioning. The three models presented each help increase comprehension of the complex interrelated systems that affect learning:
1. up-and-down or evolutionary and reticular activating system model
2. side-by-side or hemispheric brain model
3. connections or programs of the brain model

Up-and-Down Models

Stellar (1954) presented one of the first up-and-down models of the brain. He viewed the cortex as possessing a steering function for behavior and the midbrain as having a starting/stopping function. An automobile steering wheel might represent the cortex and brain

---

[1] Broca's area is the portion of the frontal lobe of the cerebral cortex (see brain diagram, p. 7) in the left hemisphere of most people which, when damaged, results in loss of the ability to speak. The speech loss from damage to this area has more to do with motor control of words and language sequencing than with conceptual aspects of language. This area is named for Paul Broca, a noted French pathologist and surgeon who in 1861 first postulated the localized function of this area. His theories were developed primarily as a result of postmortem studies of the brains of individuals who had experienced loss of ability to speak after trauma or disease.

Wernicke's area is the portion of the temporal lobe of the cerebral cortex (see brain diagram, p. 7) in the left hemisphere of most people which, when damaged, results in loss of the ability to understand spoken and written language. A person suffering from damage to this area may be able to speak and write distinctly and rapidly but with little connected expression of ideas or evidence of comprehension. The area is named for Carl Wernicke, a German physician who in 1874 established a theory that made it possible to predict symptoms that would result from damage to specific regions of the cortex.

The theories advanced by Paul Broca in 1861 and Carl Wernicke in 1874 have had far-reaching effects in the fields of brain function, neuropsychology, neuroanatomy, and neurosurgery. The theories are still held to be true today in terms of symptomatic results of damage to specific regions of the cortex; however, debate exists over the reasons that damage to certain regions of the brain results in certain symptoms. Radiating functional communications and loss of a balancing of facilitation and inhibition functions are among the alternate explanations.

stem while the accelerator and brake pedal would be the limbic system. Though simplistic, the model broke with prevailing notions of the cortex as the sole executive of the neurological system. Stellar pointed to the important ascending and descending communications between brain structures and the pivotal role of the limbic system in deciding the actions of the brain and the body.

MacLean (1978) called his more complete up-and-down model the triune, or three-part brain. In relating the old brain stem, middle limbic system, and new cortex, he found that the developing complexity of the human nervous system parallels that of animal brains on the phlogenetic scale.

The brain stem of the human brain, which MacLean (1978) called the Reptilian complex (R-complex), resembles reptilian brains in structure and function. The R-complex handles primary survival instincts: obtaining food, finding and guarding territories or homesites, ritual courting and mating, and social routines such as greeting and migration. Although the human brain stem and cerebellum carry out automatic motor and life-support functions, survival responses are also affected by the next highest structure, the limbic system.

The brain automatically adjusts body functions to respond to different situations and activities with hormones. Homeostasis is a major responsibility of the organs in the midbrain. When a person runs, the heart speeds up, respiration increases, and body temperature is controlled through perspiration. Hunger and thirst activate drives to satisfy needs. Danger or threat flood the body with hormones that temporarily increase alertness and strength. Physiological reactions to exertion, thirst, and fear differ only slightly from the physiological reactions that accompany emotional response to a wide range of situations. The limbic system hormones control both reactions.

The uppermost brain structures in the cortex handle the broadly defined function of thinking. The neocortex, or simply the new brain, enables humans to decide how to respond to situations, use language, plan for the future, and look consciously at those thought processes. How *homo sapiens* developed such a powerful tool as the new brain continues to be a fascinating mystery. Many clues point to a selective process that allowed hominid ancestors to survive by outsmarting other stronger, faster, and fiercer beasts (Jerison 1977; Sagan 1977; MacLean 1978).

The functioning of the reticular activating system (RAS) suggests another up-and-down model of the brain. The role of the RAS in general arousal and attention has been investigated extensively for the past 20 years in animal and sensory deprivation studies (Buck

1976). General arousal appears to be an underlying aspect of an elaborate decision-making process in the brain involving virtually all brain structures in an ascending and descending communication network. Sensory information first goes to the RAS in the brain stem and then upward to the specific sensory and broader association areas of the cortex. Not all sensory information is responded to equally because of selective gating all along the reticular system (Young 1978). Otherwise, humans might drown in a deluge of sensory stimulation.

Response such as removing a finger from a hot stove may need only the reflexive motor control low in the nervous system. Adjusting to heat or cold requires the higher level of the midbrain homeostatic mechanism. Confrontation with new information calls on the associative capacity of the cortex. Rowe (1978) suggests that the importance of discrepance or surprise in classroom settings is due to their ability to open the RAS gates.

The up-and-down models of the brain—Stellar, evolutionary, and reticular activating system—agree on two dominant themes: the function of higher and lower structures and the interrelatedness of their actions. Maslow's hierarchy of needs (1954) is a more familiar schema that suggests a similar hierarchy of behavioral relationships. These brain models support child development goals of physical and self-esteem growth as prerequisite and integral parts of educating young children.

Side-by-Side Models

The bilateral symmetry of the brain suggests another view of brain functioning. The hemispheric model began in 1846 with Broca's work with stroke and brain-damaged patients. Broca found that language deficits were associated with damage to the left hemisphere. Work by Sperry and his associates (Sperry, Gazzaniga, and Bogen 1969) provided dramatic evidence that two separate thinking systems characterize cortical functioning. The hemispheres are joined by a communication network consisting largely of the corpus callosum. The corpus callosum of each of several epileptic patients was surgically cut to prevent transmission of the electrical disturbance from one side to the other. Because the hemispheres of the brain are connected to the opposite sides of the body for sensory input and motor control, information presented to the left ear, left hand, and left visual field of each eye goes to the right hemisphere and vice versa. For the split-brain patients, the information sent to one hemisphere could not travel across the corpus callosum to inform the other side of the brain. One side of the brain and its half of the body did not know what the other half was doing.

Ingenious experiments were used by the brain investigators to examine the special abilities of the two hemispheres. For example, in one such experiment, split-brain patients were given objects to feel separately with either the right or left hand. A subject's own hands and the objects to be felt were shielded from the subject's sight. When the left hand (right hemisphere) was presented a cutout numeral to feel, the person could indicate the value of the numeral with fingers, but only with the left hand. When asked to name the object or show the value with the right hand (left hemisphere), the person could only guess. Even though the right hemisphere could not verbally describe a cup presented to the left hand, it could find the cup again. The right hemisphere was mute but not ignorant, as had sometimes been thought.

In another study, Levy, Trevarthen, and Sperry (1972) had split-brain subjects memorize the pictures and names of eight people. The subjects then were asked to identify pictures which were actually combined halves (chimera) of two of the faces already associated with names. The subjects watched a dot in the center of a screen. Then a chimera picture was flashed for a tenth of a second—too short a time for the eyes to scan across the picture. Thus, each brain hemisphere saw only half of the picture. When asked to identify the person's face by pointing, the subjects found the face which had occupied the left visual space (right hemisphere). However, when the subjects were asked to name the face they had seen, they named the person seen in the right visual field—information that had been received by the left hemisphere. Results from dozens of studies (Wittrock 1978b) revealed a pattern of strengths demonstrated by the two halves of the brain. These studies found that in a majority of people the left hemisphere tends to operate as an analytic specialist and a detailed and sequential builder of ideas; it is best able to store or retrieve information in a part-by-part coded form such as words. The right hemisphere in most people tends to work as a specialist in understanding an entire idea and filling in the necessary missing gaps; it is prone to store or retrieve information in a spatial manner such as pictures or images.

The importance of split-brain discoveries might have been limited if work had not also been continued with people having an intact corpus callosum. To assess hemispheric processing in normal adults and children, experiments were devised in which individuals were asked to respond to stimuli presented simultaneously to the two hemispheres via contralateral connections from the right and left hand, right and left ear, or right and left visual half-field. Assumptions underlying this research technique imply that simultaneous presentation to the two brain hemispheres will cause competition between them and that the hemisphere which has a thinking style best suited to the task will perform better. For a comprehensive review of these data, see Wittrock (1978b), Chall and Mirsky (1978), Harnad (1977), and Kraft (in press). The following examples are illustrative of a large research literature.

Kimura (1961) employed a dichotic listening technique in which competing signals were directed simultaneously to each ear. When numbers were used as stimuli, the left hemisphere/right ear was more accurate. However, when environmental sounds were used, the right hemisphere/left ear was more accurate (Knox and Kimura 1970). These findings point to the verbal speciality of the left hemisphere while suggesting that auditory input of less verbally coded information is handled best by the right hemisphere. Witelson (1977) used the sense of touch in dichaptic tests. When right-handed children reached into a curtained box and explored irregular shapes with fingers of each hand, the left hand was more accurate at identifying shapes. Thus, the spatial strength of the right hemisphere was demonstrated in normal people. The experiments show a tendency for each hemisphere to be better at certain tasks presented in certain ways consistent with the split-brain findings. The electroencephalogram (EEG), another research technique, records and analyzes brain waves while individuals perform tasks. EEG studies show that while a subject is doing a verbal task such as writing a letter or taking notes, alpha waves (which indicate brain idling) are more prevalent in the right hemisphere and beta waves (which indicate higher level cognitive processing) are more prevalent in the left hemisphere. During a spatial task, such as constructing a block design, the pattern of brain waves is reversed (Galin and Ornstein 1975).

All these studies could be and sometimes have been misinterpreted to mean language is a completely left-brain activity or art is an entirely right-brain one. This incorrect interpretation misses the main point of hemispheric brain functioning and learning: Hemispheric brain functioning emphasizes differences in processing. The two hemispheres extract different aspects of meaning from the same experience. In appreciating a painting, both overall color and contour and specific features are assessed. Music has a recognizable melody even when details such as key and tempo are changed. Mathematics uses specific symbols and linear operations to express largely spatial relationships.

The two hemispheres generate unitary inner experiences by providing two points of view on external experiences. The corpus callosum and other connections allow interhemispheric communication for comparing and evaluating the knowledge of each side. People have the capacity to engage both the analytic and emotional, verbal and visuo-spatial, and sequential and simultaneous modes.

However, the mode actually used depends on many variables. Personal preference or intention, salient features of experience, instructions, habitual reliance on one type—all may determine which processing style takes the lead. One side may dominate the reception and the response without the check and balance of complementary processing. Integrated experience for meaningful learning is one clear educational implication of the hemispheric model.

The side-by-side model provides a foundation for a new appreciation and assessment of individual differences. Differences may arise from (1) predominant processing styles of individuals and their ability to adapt processing appropriately, (2) experiences that enhance or inhibit integration of processing, or (3) dynamic interaction of processing styles and experience.

Connection Models

The inner workings of the brain that result in behavior provide another set of questions, research directions, and models of brain functioning. Hebb (1949) suggested that pathways connecting certain cells are strengthened by experience resulting in cell assemblies. In the 30 years since Hebb's work, the idea of connection in the brain has been pursued in two ways. Neurochemistry deals with actual neuronal linkages and describes the function of neurotransmitters in facilitating or inhibiting brain connections. The other approach suggests programs of behavior resulting from neuronal operation. The two approaches provide a microcosmic and a macrocosmic view of how functional connections and patterns are established in the brain.

The microstructure of the brain hints at the intricate and complex nature of neurochemical connection. In addition to cells found in all tissue, two distinctive types of cells are found in the brain: neuron or nerve cells and glial cells. Neurons act on one another electrically and chemically and interact with glial cells, possibly exchanging nutrients as well as ions.

A synapse, the point of interaction between neurons, is actually a gap between the sending mechanism of one cell and the receiving mechanism of another. What is exchanged at synaptic sites are neurochemical transmitter substances including hormones, enzymes, and peptides. Advanced technology in magnification, photography, and computer analysis allows investigation of the powerful effects of transmitter substances on behavior. Such studies yield (1) knowledge about specific substances and their function in the nervous system, (2) understanding of the ways in which drugs work to mimic or interrupt natural neural processes, and (3) insight into the complexity of actions and interactions of structures and substances in the brain.

The complexity of neural connections points not only to intricate neurochemical interactions but also to the immense number of cells. Each of the approximately 12 billion neurons in the human brain has up to 5,000 synapses. The number of possible interconnections in the brain is larger than the number of atomic particles in the universe (Thompson 1975). All growth, structural development, and functional activity involves either transmission or change in the myriad chemical connections. Clearly, meaningful brain activity in the usual sense does not occur when one neuron fires; neither does brain functioning characteristically involve activity in all the billions of neurons. Instead, neurons seem to be activated in groups and sequences.

The processes associating neurochemical connections with behaviors have been compared to computer programs or telephone switchboards. Such hard-wired programs might be appropriate for describing instinctual responses of the lower brain, but they are limited for describing individuality in learning and thinking. Hebb's cell assemblies (1949) link neurochemical function and behavior in an early model of brain programs. Thus, Hebb's model marks movement from an inert to a dynamic model of brain function.

In Hebb's model, varied and associated experiences result in networks of related cell assemblies. These cell assemblies make generalized responses possible; for example, people learn many forms of triangles, chairs, and friendship. Programs allow recognition, elaboration, and even anticipation of life situations.

Prosters [Hart's (1975) version of programs] serve as templates that the brain uses as it quickly scans its repertoire. The main features of a current experience are compared with existing prosters. When the two match, response is practically automatic and unconscious. Expectations that are met do not require adjustments; however, events that have no preexisting proster events cannot be matched. Hart stated that the brain's ability to deal with newness is impaired under threat or extreme emotion. The reticular activating system downshifts to older, lower preprograms that prevent new connections and new learning.

Several aspects of the three brain models already discussed are treated from a functional point of view by Luria (1973). Luria proposed three functional blocks of the brain, each with a structural component. Block one consists of the upper and lower brain stem, the ascending and descending pathways in the reticular formation, and the hippocampus. It is responsible for arousal and the waking state of the cortex. Ascending nerves carry messages which excite and activate the cortex while descending messages inhibit and subordinate lower structures to programs arising in the cortex. Block two is located in the occipital, parietal, and temporal lobes of the right and left hemispheres and is functionally related to obtaining, processing, and storing information. Each block also has three levels of functional organization: primary, secondary, and tertiary levels. In block two the functions become increasingly lateralized at secondary and tertiary levels. Block three is located in the neocortex and consists of the frontal lobes. It is functionally responsible for formulating plans and intentions and for developing brain programs which organize, integrate, regulate, and control other parts of the cortex and lower brain structures.

Memory becomes important in the concept of brain programs. What is memory and where is it? Pribram (1971) speculated that memory works like a photographic hologram in which experience is stored throughout the brain. As early as 1935, Lashley suggested that no evidence exists for localized engram storage in either of the hemispheres. Meyer and Meyer (forthcoming) pursued this notion in 20 years of comparative experimental animal studies. They stated that efforts to "bake, burn, freeze, and cut" memories from the cortex have failed and that no injury through which the individual can survive destroys memory completely. They proposed the hypothalamus as the likely site of storage and stressed that damage to the cortex results in loss of ability to retrieve the memory, not in loss of the memory itself.

Despite the difficulty of locating the site of the memory, Young (1978) suggested that the effects of coded and stored memory are evident in all human behavior. He proposed several levels of brain programs which "are a most intricate set of plans and arrangements . . . which have been constructed from influences, some recent, some from long, long ago (p. 11)." DNA genetic preprogramming determines individual characteristics such as hair color and body shape. Evolutionary characteristics of the species, including brain structure, represent another preprogram level.

The dynamic program that distinguishes humans is their capacity to learn from experience. Planning, based upon goal-directed, selective, and intentional programs, guides all parts of human behavior. While other animals have the capacity to learn, only people have developed access to cultural and historical programs or memory outside the body. Recorded thought from cave drawings to computer storage capacity provides resources for choosing actions with a perspective beyond the present.

Young stated that his model was hypothetical about brain programs but that he was certain of four elements of brain functioning:
1. The brain responds to uniquely human characteristics such as the human voice and facial configuration.
2. The brain can establish elaborate abstract coding systems such as language and mathematical symbolism.

3. The brain deals with the world systematically.
4. The brain works as an integrated whole.

Understanding the integrated brain provides a foundation for understanding all aspects of human behavior, including learning and emotions.

Suggested Readings

Boddy, J. *Brain Systems and Psychological Concepts.* New York: Wiley, 1978.
Chall, J. S., and Mirsky, A. F. *Education and the Brain.* 77th National Society for the Study of Education Yearbook, Part II. Chicago: University of Chicago Press, 1978.
Hart, L. A. *How the Brain Works.* New York: Basic Books, 1975.
Restak, R. M. *The Brain: The Last Frontier.* Garden City, N.Y.: Doubleday, 1979.
Sagan, C. *The Dragons of Eden.* New York: Ballantine, 1977.
Teyler, T. J. *A Primer of Psychobiology.* San Francisco: Freeman, 1975.
Uttal, W. R. *Psychobiology of Mind.* Hillsdale, N.J.: Lawrence Erlbaum Associates, 1978.
Wittrock, M. C. *The Human Brain.* Englewood Cliffs, N.J.: Prentice-Hall, 1977.
Young, J. Z. *Programs of the Brain.* Oxford: University of Oxford Press, 1978.

II

Brain Functioning: The Study of the Learning Processes

Young children show substantial gains in verbal fluency, language complexity, and logic when they engage in activity-based, inquiry-oriented science programs.

3
Individuals and Language Development

Language provides a means for understanding learning processes and serves as a curriculum area for applying what we know and are discovering about learning. Three established areas of inquiry suggest a framework for the future study of language development in early childhood education:
1. inquiry into the motor component of establishing meaning
2. inquiry into the role of extended child monologues in language growth
3. inquiry into early conceptions of print and sound representations

Motoric Development of Meaning

Weaving a system of meanings must precede the verbal use of a language system. Activity, motor involvement, and play are significant in the establishment of a language system (Carter 1975; Cazden 1974). Bruner (1975) postulated that language was not an innate mechanism but, instead, is acquired to regulate joint activity and attention.

Numerous studies of children's early utterances (Bates 1976; Bloom 1973; Corrigan 1976; Greenfield and Smith 1976; Harding and Golingkoff 1977; Ingram 1976; Lezine 1973; Raph and Nicholich 1975; Dihoff and Chapman 1977; Carter 1975) support the idea that verbally expressed meanings are constructed through action before utterance. Hemispheric brain function theory also supports the primacy of development of motor meanings. Kinsbourne (1978) noted that lateral orienting is evident in the behavioral repertoire of the newborn human infant. In the babbling stages of language acquisition, vocalization occurs first in conjunction with lateral orienting and then with locomotion, grasping, and manipulation. Kinsbourne further observed that infants vocalize or babble while engaged in action before they have learned which conventional verbal signals are associated with what events; superficial elements of language develop before complete cognitive language processing occurs.

New forms eventually express previously established motor meanings, and thus new words are abstract labels for cognitively old content. Labeling motorically established meanings serves a variety of functions. For example, once a child has labeled the concept of *here* as meaning *close to me*, the single word utterance of "here" can serve a summoning function meaning "Mommy come here; I need you"; an offering function meaning "Here, you take this sticky lollipop. I don't want it anymore"; or a placing function meaning "Here is the shoe we were looking for all morning."

Teaching Implications

With the notion of language functions and language uses comes children's abilities to form hypotheses about the rules functioning within their language environment. Many current early childhood language programs focus on hypothesizing, testing, refining, and finally moving toward conventional adult speech.

Active manipulation of the physical world curriculum implies creating an environment favorable for the establishment of motoric representations. Rowe (1978) observed that young children show substantial gains in verbal fluency, language complexity, and logic when they engage in activity-based, inquiry-oriented science programs as a language builder. The inner-city children involved in the Rowe study showed 200 percent to 500 percent more student-initiated, content-relevant speech during science lessons than during language arts lessons.

In early childhood education, such a program is especially significant because of the sensitive sensory, motor, and cognitive learning characteristics of the very young child. A two and a half-year-old child who bends his chin and draws his hand as though it were a bow across his other outstretched arm while talking about the instrument his older sister plays knows the meaning of *violin*. A three-year-old child who slowly, carefully pulls up an invisible string while talking about catching crabs at the shore knows the meaning of *crabbing*.

Play is an obvious element in establishing motoric meanings. In play situations, children freely explore and establish concepts without the risk of being wrong. An activity-based curriculum should become the foundation of an integrated language development program. Children's language growth flows from internally established meanings. Although carefully observing and recording individual and interactional children's language does provide insights into children's cognitive and linguistic development, such observations do not provide the whole picture of what children know, are capable of knowing, or are capable of doing.

Informed early childhood educators will refrain from judging a child's intellectual ability or knowledge based on verbal output. Instead, they will facilitate establishment of motoric meanings and the use of language playfully, without risk. This use of language draws a child's attention to communication. The educator then becomes an interpreting adult who listens carefully and engages a child in extending linguistic rules through analogy with already internalized rules of action.

Sustaining Independent Speech

Britton (1970) suggested that the appearance of the extended monologue (talk sustained without outside verbal stimuli) in a child's speech marks the earliest step in the ability to communicate through writing. Such a suggestion seems incongruous because early childhood educators have been trained to look for socialized language as a significant step indicating developmental growth. One senses that many teachers are currently seeking to eliminate or lessen the proportion of egocentric speech compared to socialized speech in their young students so as to facilitate growth. Educators have often placed children in situations in which most of the evolving communication revolves around taking turns. For example, the teacher asks; the child responds; and the teacher asks a follow-up question or makes a summary or judgmental statement. By maintaining the ability to question, the teacher holds power and control to continue or terminate the interaction situation.

If we examine Britton's viewpoint, young children who spontaneously engage in extended monologues are engaged in a language activity closely related to narrative writing; they are verbally pursuing their own patterns of relationships and stores of meanings. It is likely that children who engage in extended monologues have also been engaged in inner speech and imaging. Graves (1978) in studying the writing process, noted the importance of the incubation stage. During this stage writers search their store of knowledge and image the relationships between personal meanings and the task at hand. Perhaps when young children think in images and are provided with time and stimulus for doing so, their encounters with the incubation stage in later writing tasks could be facilitated.

Teaching Implications

Early childhood programs evolving from this postulated relationship between the appearance of extended monologues and the writing process should focus on the significant role of the adult as an involved, active listener. Current programs stress developing listening skills in the child. Future programs should stress developing listening skills in the educator. Even if one disagrees with the relationship suggested between monologues and writing, the involved adult listener certainly would provide a positive model for the child. The sensitive teacher can increase knowledge about individual children and about improving the learning environment through active listening. There are, for example, educationally important differences among children who describe similar experiences as having been nice and funny, fantastic and thrilling, or unhappy and scary.

If the educator is to listen, the spatial, temporal, and curricular organization of the early childhood program must provide opportunities for extended talk. First, the teacher should actively involve children in experiences about which to talk and then reduce the number of questions, especially convergent ones, asked of young children actively engaged in learning (Cunningham 1977). Finally, the teacher should increase the amount of waiting time provided for answering children's divergent questions (Rowe 1978).

In addition, an awareness of culturally significant rules for who is supposed to talk to whom, when it is appropriate to talk, and what it is proper to talk about is essential if the teacher and child are from culturally different backgrounds (DeStefano 1978). Answers to children's questions should facilitate understanding beyond the words used to respond. Perkes (1971) suggested that reducing knowing to words limits creativity and restricts understanding. Teachers of young children must be careful not to close off inquiry with explanations because children need to play words back against experience.

Early Conceptions of Sound and Print Representation

Early conceptions of print and spelling suggest a relationship between monologues and writing. Read (1975) and Clay (1975) conducted fascinating investigations of young children actively exploring spelling and writing systems and formed hypotheses about the rules and regularities governing such systems. Both researchers presented evidence that many young children exposed to print demonstrate developmentally increasing systematic awareness of those "written down" aspects of their language. To an untrained eye a young child's production of "YSAPNTIALGTIGO" bears little resemblance to the traditional literary beginning: "Once upon a time, a long time ago." It is even harder to recognize that a newly painted kitchen wall proudly adorned with crayon marks resembling somewhat vertically arranged strands of spaghetti may indicate that the very young child is exploring the linear aspects she or he has already

Teachers should actively involve children in experiences about which to talk and then reduce the number of convergent questions they ask.

perceived in print. The Read and Clay inquiries into spontaneous spellings and print exploration indicate that such is the case and that many children between the ages of three and six are actively involved in making sense of the written aspect of the language environment.

Teaching Implications

Mainstream American society strongly believes that success in the early grades equals success in mastering tasks associated with reading and writing instruction. It is unfortunate when early childhood programs ignore both the interest many young children have in creatively manipulating the writing system and their internalized knowledge of this system. It is ironic that children who have managed to maintain and advance their control of the writing system are pressured to ignore what they already know when they enter first grade. They must start at the beginning because "now they are ready," according to a reading program.

Teachers can encourage children who are interested in exploring print and spelling. Such explorations and self-seeking of regularities enhance later linguistic growth. Much as play with verbal aspects of language yields essential practice without debilitating risks, play with the written aspects of language enables the child to evolve a risk-free environment in which to master subtle aspects of form.

Correctness or incorrectness of such experimentation should not be the immediate concern of the educator, for the young learner is already moving toward conventional forms. Early childhood educators should look for consistencies in the ways children spontaneously deal with acquisition of the written language. Children who deal with language forms in this concrete manner paradoxically become aware of the abstractness of language. Such metalinguistic awareness is necessary in the reading process (Cazden 1974; Klima 1972; and Mattingly 1972). It cannot be assumed that all children in an early childhood program will be interested in exploring print and orthography. However, the consistencies demonstrated by those who are interested and involved may yield valuable information concerning what children naturally abstract about the reading and writing process as compared to formal literacy instruction.

Thus, the current emphasis in research on child language acquisition suggests patterns for future early childhood education language development programs. Such patterns emphasize—

- building opportunities for motoric development of meanings in advance of and simultaneous with verbal, semantic expectations;
- recognizing that what a child can say and what a child can do or can know are not equivalent;
- providing opportunities for young children to engage in extended monologues with adults who serve not as questioners but as involved, active listeners; and
- evolving educator sensitivity to children's systematic attempts at spontaneously gaining access to print and/or orthography.

These patterns indicate the importance of providing low-risk opportunities for those children interested in engaging in print or spelling exploration. Attention to these four implications of language development may lead to knowledge relating natural aspects of learning to later formal conventions of reading and writing.

Suggested Readings

Cazden, C. B. *Child Language and Education*. New York: Holt, Rinehart & Winston, 1972.
Clay, M. H. *What Did I Write?* New York: International Publications Service, 1975.
DeVilliers, J. G., and DeVilliers, P. A. *Language Acquisition*. Cambridge, Mass.: Harvard University Press, 1978.
Donaldson, M. *Children's Minds*. London: Fontana/Collins, 1978.
Goodman, M. E. *The Culture of Childhood, Child's Eye View of Society and Culture*. New York: Teachers College Press, Columbia University, 1970.
Ingram, D. "Sensorimotor Intelligence and Language Development." In *Action, Gesture, and Symbol: The Emergence of Language*, ed. A. Lock. New York: Academic Press, 1976.
Vygotsky, L. S. *Thought and Language*. Cambridge, Mass.: MIT Press, 1962.

Parent education might benefit from focusing on the developing adult and on aspects of adult development as antecedents of parenting behavior.

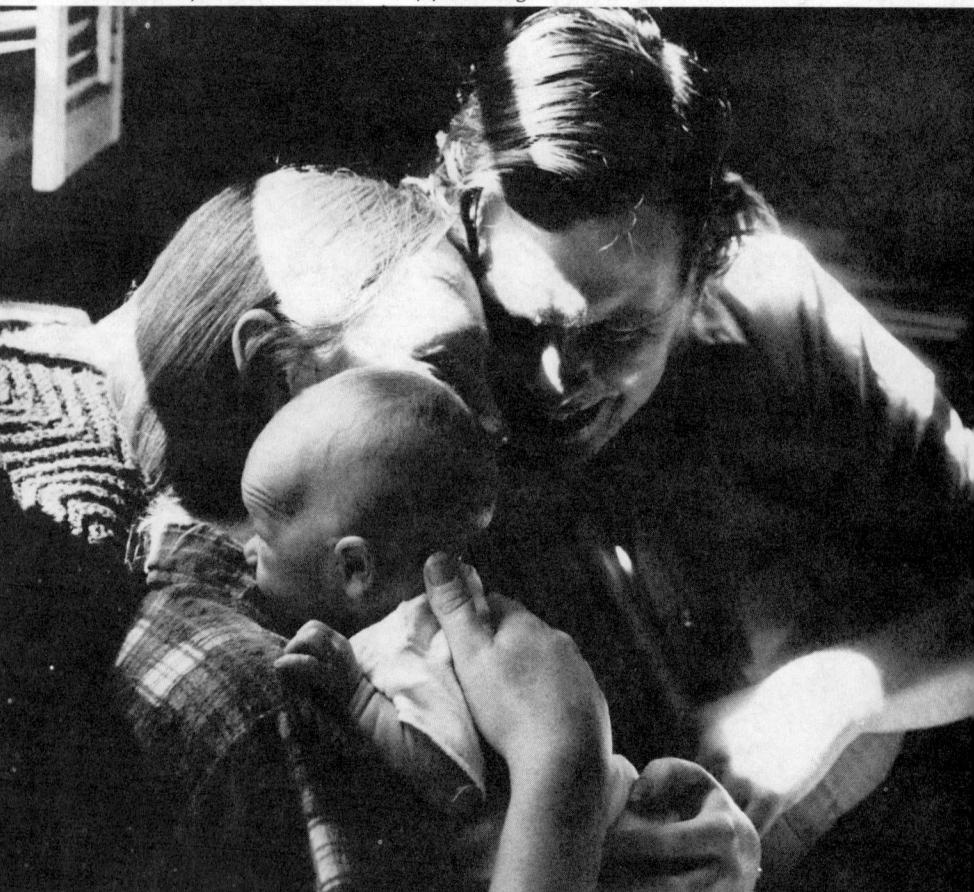

4
Individuals and Development

Human development holds a respected position in the theoretical and conceptual models of early childhood education. Four strands of human development that may influence the future of early childhood education relate brain functioning and developmental components of an individual's learning style.

Life-Span Development

Human development models are characterized by qualitatively different stages through which an individual proceeds in an invariant sequence. Much of the stage development work has produced age-bracketed and relatively isolated specialities (Baltes and Willis 1979).

Recent work in adult development (Levinson 1978; Lowenthal et al. 1975; Gould 1978) reveals that stages of human development, often assumed to be completed during adolescence, continue throughout the life span. Not only are there predictable, qualitatively different stages during adult life, but the transitions between them are rather sensitive times. Riegel (1975) proposed a human development dialectic in which interactions between the inner biological, psychological, cultural/sociological, and physical/environmental dimensions are central. Positive resolution of conflict leads to growth while failure prevents progress in development.

Just as young children continually develop in various areas, their important adults (teachers, parents) also change developmentally. The interaction of these adult-child developmental lines provides a model for study and application in early childhood learning in the home and school.

Developmental factors throughout life clearly influence the emergence of learning, teaching, and parenting styles in individuals. An individual's characteristic behavior as a learner, teacher, or parent partly depends on the individual's developmental lifeline. Each person's style changes with the stresses and strains of movement along the developmental lifeline. The quality of interpersonal transactions reflects these developmentally influenced style changes and the nature of the matches and mismatches that occur between people at various points.

Teaching Implications

In addition to linkage between the unfolding of learning, teaching, and parenting styles and life-span development, a life-span development perspective can be applied to other areas concerning early childhood educators. First, parent education might benefit from focusing on the developing adult and on aspects of adult development as antecedents of parenting behavior. The life-span development model may help both family therapists and their clients in critical areas of parenting, such as child abuse. Such people may find it useful to examine the stresses and strains that lead to violence according to the developmental lifelines of everyone involved. Concerned individuals should recognize that eventually both adults and children will be under different developmental influences.

Brain development partly affects these developmental influences. For example, the two-year-old child may irritate her parents by orally repeating "no" to the parent's directive, while continuing to toddle relentlessly toward Aunt Martha's fragile antique vase. Neurologically at this age, the child's spatial right and verbal left hemisphere do not yet communicate well. Later the corpus callosum will function more efficiently. We might respond less emotionally to the two-year-old child if we understood a bit more about brain development.

At the other end of the life span, the brain changes somewhat during senescence. Hebb (1978) commented sensitively on changes he observed in his own memory and brain function at 72. For example, a melody recalled in the morning might "play" again and again throughout the day, as though the responsible cell assembly continued to recycle in his short-term memory. The brain functioning development perspective helps us empathize and understand conscious mental life for the elderly.

A life-span development view expanded by knowledge of brain functioning may also stimulate early childhood educators to expand programs bringing together the elderly and young children. The complementary differences in life-span development of these two age groups, for example, can be used in surrogate grandparent and grandchild roles, often missing in our mobile culture.

Finally, it may be useful to investigate relationships between the career development of early childhood educators and life-span development features of those same individuals, their colleagues, and families. Katz (1977) and Fuller and Bowen (1975) began work in this direction. Investigations of deep personality structures, such as work on ego development by Loevinger (1976) and locus of control summarized by Lefcourt (1976), suggest a context from which to view career development, role adequacy, and job satisfaction.

Sensitive Periods

A sensitive period occurs when the individual undergoes a developmental transition and approaches new experiences or familiar situations differently. The individual, more easily influenced than usual, exhibits a less settled and directed profile. The sensitive period concept differs from the older critical period concept that was largely built from animal studies and emphasized deficits and irreversibility associated with failure to establish certain behaviors. Leiderman (1978) pointed out that in 1962 Caldwell effectively conceptualized how to apply the sensitive period concept to a range of human studies in the behavorial sciences.

Researchers criticized some of the ensuing work on the critical period concept as oversimplified and perhaps misapplied. Recent studies of human neurological development (Chall and Mirsky 1978) vitalized the sensitive period idea and emphasized that, while the human brain is remarkably plastic and adaptable, there are optimal times to stimulate learning. These sensitive periods may partly coincide with a child's readiness for certain kinds of learning. Current thinking in sensitive periods attempts to integrate the biological, psychological, and social dimensions of the concept.

Early life has been viewed entirely as a sensitive period (Williams 1976). In the future, sensitive periods will be studied more broadly. We need to plan now to use such knowledge in schools and homes.

Many patterns of behavior may emerge in the brain. Certain patterns do become established. The somewhat timed activation of those patterns provides interesting possibilities in unraveling the mystery of how individual differences emerge.

This view considers learning basically a matter of selection among the many possible pathways in the brain. Unwanted, unused pathways would functionally disappear, and those chosen would improve by use. Thus, we recognize—

> . . . a series of sensitive periods in development at each of which the brain, with appropriate input, develops certain of its features . . . The evidence is, of course, easiest to come by for earlier states, but it may well be that the emergence of new possibilities continues far into life . . . even to our final decades . . . and thus relates to the problems of senescence. (Young 1978, p.27)

MacLean (1978) postulated a sensitive period for the development of the emotion of empathy corresponding to the maturation of structures in the limbic brain and frontal lobes. Yarrow and Waxler

(1975) provided empirical evidence generally supporting an altruistic orientation of young children that matches the sensitive period MacLean suggested. This evidence about developmental aspects of altruism does not conflict with the Piagetian notion that young children tend toward cognitively centered and egocentric thinking. It does caution us to avoid generalizing from cognitive features to affective capabilities of young children, such as altruism, which may be strongly influenced by limbic brain structures. In her anthropologically oriented work with young learners, Goodman (1971) proposed that complex social interactions characterize early life.

In an area not yet fully researched, Epstein (1978) correlated brain growth spurts with Piagetian stages and postulated another stage, problem finding, beyond Piaget's formal operations. Epstein suggested that times of rapid brain growth mostly associated with growth of glial cells, myelination, and dendritic branching are sensitive periods when new learning might be introduced. Times of slow brain growth might be times to limit new cognitive input and consolidate existing concepts. Ideas that hold promise to enrich and extend Piagetian theory in the years ahead are emerging from biologically based sciences—the same area in which Piaget was trained.

Neurological Development

The orientation of the young child to visuo-spatial and motor experiences suggests the primacy of a right brain learning style in early life (Harris 1976; Kraft and Languis 1977). Kraft (1976) conducted an EEG study of six- to eight-year-old children while they performed Piagetian conservation-of-substance tasks. Across subjects, beta wave activity was higher in the right hemisphere during visuo-spatial manipulation of materials and in the left hemisphere during verbal explanation of equivalence. But subjects who achieved conservation had more balanced brain wave activity between the hemispheres during both parts of the tasks. Kraft interpreted her data to suggest that myelination of the fibers of the corpus callosum connecting the right and left hemispheres occurs at about the same age that Piagetian conservation and reversibility are achieved. Thus, more efficient hemispheric communication is associated with the achievement of conservation in Piagetian tasks.

Galin et al. (1979) asked three- and five-year-old children to judge whether textures touched simultaneously with each hand were the same or different. Because each brain hemisphere received different information simultaneously, Galin reasoned that communication between the hemispheres would be required for subjects to make

We might respond less emotionally to the two-year-old if we understood a bit more about brain development.

accurate judgments. The results showed that five-year-old children were considerably more accurate than three-year-old children, thus providing supportive empirical evidence for the myelination cycle and improved interhemispheric communication hypothesis Kraft proposed.

Motor learning seems to form the basis of meaning in early child language as shown when a young child repeats the physical movements of an experience while attempting to express the experience verbally. This also seems to support teachers' observations about

31

personal meanings that accompany verbal descriptions of created pictures, art objects, and active fantasy and role play (Wolfgang 1977; Smilansky 1968). Moreover, Cook-Gumperz and Gumperz (1978) found that children displayed wide variation in register during play situations. (Registers are language varieties determined by the social circumstances of their use; thus the children involved actively in play evidenced a social awareness beyond the scope of their typical language.) New experiences that are relatively uncoded or for which no labels exist may be processed primarily in the right hemisphere. With repetition and additional encounters, appropriate codes develop in the left hemisphere as the processing switches from right to left (Krashen 1977).

Albert and Obler investigated neurological organization in first- and second-language learning with comparisons of aphasia in right or left hemisphere trauma of monolinguals and bilinguals. They suggested that "the right hemisphere plays a major role in the acquisition of a second language, at any age . . . " and "it might be useful to teach a second language using so-called 'right-hemisphere strategies' such as nursery rhymes, music, dance, and techniques using visuo-spatial skills (Albert and Obler 1978, p. 254)." All language learning may reflect a right hemisphere base, followed by more linear sequential left hemisphere emphases as verbal fluency emerges. For example, the rhythmic repetitions, such as da-da-da, often accompanied by correspondingly patterned limb movements, focus on high imagery nouns and verbs of early child talk—all right hemisphere features of speech. The typical stage-specific appearance of overgeneralizations of language rules indicates that young children have extensive, broad knowledge about language. Such global understanding reflects right hemisphere aspects of knowing. Moreover, Searlman's (1977) critical review of the right hemisphere's role in linguistic functions documents the strength of the right hemisphere's role in comprehension of speech and print.

Considering the various threads emerging from developmental neurology and linguistic research and theory, it may be appropriate to build from existing developmental learning theories, such as Piaget's, to new theoretical constructs.

Suggested Readings

Bortner, M., ed. *Cognitive Growth and Development*. New York: Brunner/Mazel, 1978.
Diamond, S. J., and Beaumont, J. G., eds. *Hemisphere Function in the Human Brain*. New York: Wiley, 1974.
Donaldson, M. *Children's Minds*. New York: Norton, 1978.
Eliot, J., and Salkind, N. J., eds. *Children's Spatial Development*. Springfield, Ill.: Charles C. Thomas, 1975.

Grenell, R. G., and Gabay, S., eds. *Biological Foundations of Psychiatry*, Vols. I and II. New York: Raven Press, 1976.

Horowitz, F. D. *Early Developmental Hazards: Predictors and Precautions*. Volume 19, American Association for the Advancement of Science Selected Symposium. Washington, D.C.: American Association for the Advancement of Science, 1978.

Kinsbourne, M., ed. *The Asymmetrical Function of the Brain*. Cambridge: Cambridge University Press, 1976.

Knights, R. M., and Bakker, D. J. *The Neuropsychology of Learning Disorders: Theoretical Approaches*. Baltimore: University Park Press, 1976.

Kogan, N. *Cognitive Styles in Infancy and Early Childhood*. Hillsdale, N.J.: Lawrence Erlbaum Associates, 1976.

Levinson, D. J. *The Seasons of a Man's Life*. New York: Knopf, 1978.

Lowenthal, M. F.; Thurnhe, M.; and Chiriboga, D. C. *Four Stages of Life: A Comparative Study of Women and Men Facing Transitions*. New York: Jossey-Bass, 1975.

When there is an element of surprise, discrepance, or novelty in the learning environment, a surge of attention, curiosity, and interest is a natural response of the brain system to deal with the stimulating experience.

5
Individuals, Environment, and Experiences

Educators often assume that by the teacher's efforts alone children can learn anything. Focusing on the generative process of learning and the active learner presents a different position. As Hunt (1979) suggested, the interaction of the child with the environment makes the environmental conditons significant. Several aspects of the learning environment contributing to a generative model of learning are considered.

Modeling Revised

A revised view of modeling in the learning process is needed. Modeling is surely not imitation. Rather, it is a dynamic component of how young children learn many complex cognitive tasks they never "learn" formally. Models represent much of the environmental raw material children use in the learning process. Features of children's task performance resemble adult or peer performance models, thus documenting the influence of the models in children's learning.

Modeling affects attitudes and also influences the programs children build for both specific tasks and complex roles (such as parent or teacher). Modeling involves the child interacting with the performance of the task by another person; then trying to perform the task; correcting, revising, sensing rules, and overgeneralizing along the way. Modeling involves multisensory inputs that may combine with selection of certain responses from many available in the brain and gradual revision and improvement through use and social reinforcement until a reliable brain program is available for task performance.

Modeling and imagery seem to continue to play a role in the programmed expectancy used for improving or changing performance. For example, golfers may concentrate on an imagined model of the ball soaring to the pin on the green just before they drive, or divers or gymnasts may see their bodies perfectly executing complicated movements just before the event. The evidence suggests that these processes work for many people. The power of expectancy in influencing subsequent events received recent support in education contexts (Lefcourt 1976; Walker 1970). Neurological substrates may control those processes.

Much learning by young children occurs through modeling. Rice and Languis (1979) found that 10- to 12-year-old children revealed consistent superiority in assessing matches and mismatches between verbal and nonverbal classroom communication cues when the right hemisphere, compared with the left hemisphere, was presented with the cues. The subjects heard a recorded sentence with positive or negative content and inflection spoken by their own teacher. Then a picture of the teacher showing positive or negative facial expression was flashed to the right or left visual half-field (thus presenting the cue to only one hemisphere), and the subject quickly pressed a match or mismatch button. Overall performance was superior when cues were presented to the right hemisphere. The superiority of the right hemisphere was greatest when the cues had negative emotional loading. Frequently in conversations we "read between the lines" and immediately sense the relationship between the real message being communicated and the spoken words. What may be happening is that the brain, especially in the spatial right hemisphere and its parallel structure down into the limbic brain, makes a very rapid, intuitive guess about meaning in face-to-face conversation with the nonverbal cues carrying more weight than the words.

Teaching Implications

Young children often display a talent for knowing who really likes them and whom to trust. Yet both children and adults sometimes err in these judgments. Imagine the conflict a young child experiences when a parent or teacher says one thing but acts very differently. In adult-child home or classroom communication, especially where verbal and nonverbal messages are in conflict, the nonverbal modeling of meaning is likely to be chosen over words as sources of children's judgments of authenticity.

Mismatch of culturally significant cues may be a problem. For example, a teacher with a mainstream cultural background may expect a student with whom he is talking to look back straight in the eye as a sign of respectful attention. The child may be from a culture that considers a child who does not cast eyes downward when an adult is speaking to her to be disrespectful or rebellious (Williams et al. 1977). In addition, people sometimes send nonverbal messages that do not represent their actual meaning, just as we sometimes say words that do not communicate our actual ideas. Is it possible that much of what we term interpersonal effectiveness and social finesse is based on skill and accuracy in sending and receiving nonverbal communication cues? If so, this dimension of interpersonal transactions, crucial to success in roles such as teacher-student and parent-child, may be modifiable. We might look to specialists in dance and movement, mime, and drama for leadership. Teachers and students should strive toward authentic communication modeling in both verbal and nonverbal areas.

Environmental Messages

Young children are as active as adults in using environmental cues to construct reality. Brain researchers have observed that in fractions of a second the brain responds to perceived contextual cues and functionally shifts to deal with what is expected (Restak 1979; Sandman and Kastin 1977). From a neurological perspective, at the beginning of a lesson or conversation, the words, materials, organization of space, and posturing quickly induce brain activity resulting in expectancy by the child.

Teaching Implications

The quickly established set in an instructional setting probably predisposes the learning process to move in a defined direction. What may seem to be a small factor can have a large and long-lasting effect. Part of the child's motivation involves these factors. When there is an element of surprise, discrepancy, or novelty in the learning environment, a surge of attention, curiosity, and interest is a natural response of the brain system to deal with the stimulating experience. Parents and teachers have a powerful educational tool in appropriately using the arousal system of the brain.

In addition, environmental cues may be differentially attended to by individuals. The range of intragroup differences such as male-female differences typically exceeds the mean difference between the groups. Recent evidence on individual differences between the sexes (McGuiness and Pribram 1978), however, suggests that except for smell, sensory threshholds are lower for females than males. For example, females perceived sounds to be almost twice as loud and touch to be more intense than did males. Glickman and Christie (in press) found in a controlled experimental setting that compared with boys, girls were bothered more by classroom noise and performed less well on a cognitive task under noisy conditions.

McGuiness and Pribram (1978) suggested that attention to the environment due to neurological differences and cultural reinforcement is different for the sexes. Girls attend more to socially relevant, communicative dimensions while boys are more externally oriented to objects and action on the environment. Early childhood professionals might focus not only on the organization and arrangement of space and materials and to personal environmental cueing but also on the tendency of young learners to attend to different environmental messages.

Finally, the impact of the environment on the brain and learning is most apparent in the research on malnutrition and brain development. Malnutrition in the first two years of life is consistently associated with reduced brain cell growth and slowing of myelination (Winick 1976) which may be associated with developmental lags. Malnourished children often display less activity, play less, and are less curious. Restak (1979) reported a study by Chavez where during the first year of life low socioeconomic children who were given an enriched diet were six to eight times more active than comparable children in other communities. Their greater activity required more attention from the parents and substantially raised the amount of talk and emotional interactions. The Chavez data illustrate again the generative contribution of the child's behavior in the learning process.

While malnutrition manifests its influence most upon the brain development of the very young, poor nutrition and drugs also directly influence the functioning of adult brains. Undernourished children frequently have undernourished parents and siblings. In such homes, mothers and fathers often suffer from nutritionally related apathy and poor health. Food programs for children without attention to the total environment, including social conditions, will not be likely to improve the richness of environmental stimulation in the home.

Imagery

Research using rigorous controls clearly demonstrated that imagery plays an important role in language, memory, thinking, and learning and has functional characteristics that differentiate it from verbal symbolic processes (Paivio 1971, 1973; Sheehan 1972). Neuropsychological studies have further supported this view (Kimura 1966; Seamon and Gazzaniga 1973). The two processing systems represented by the right and left hemispheres of the brain—verbal-sequential on the one hand and imagery-spatial-parallel on the other—are both needed for optimal functioning (Paivio 1971; Languis and Kraft 1976, 1978).

Imagery plays an important role in problem solving (Dewing and Hetherington 1974; Stratton, Jacobus, and Leonard 1970; Wood,

Shotter, and Godden 1974; Allwood 1976; and Flaherty 1975). There is a need to establish more precisely the role of imagery in various types of concept learning (Ernest 1977). Learning science concepts often relates to problem solving. Hands-on experiences and inquiry learning in science consistently seem to involve the imagery process.

Recent studies of imagery have begun to uncover both its complexity and its potential. For example, Kosslyn (1978) found evidence of three-dimensional work space in mental images. Several types of visual imagery have been identified. Images from other sensory bases (such as sound, smell, and touch) or combinations of them not only are possible but also may contribute in important ways to memory and meaning.

Teaching Implications

After an extensive and critical view of imagery in children's learning, Pressley (1977) concluded that positive imagery effects are indisputable in a number of areas. Pictures are almost always superior to words in learning tasks. Superior reading comprehension results when children, especially so-called poor or disabled readers, form mental images from prose read or heard. Spatial imagery superiority is demonstrated especially when the task is difficult or abstract and not easily mediated by words (Ernest and Paivio 1971), but spatial imagery skill is not favored when the stimuli and encouraged response mode are verbal (Ernest 1977).

Personal use of imagery suggests drawing upon memories in numerous contexts such as sight, sound, smell, and touch. Meyer and Meyer (forthcoming) suggest that an individual's ease of access to specific memories is related to the number of different contexts or situations in which she or he has experienced that memory. If this is the case, young children could be guided to use imagery to increase their ability to draw upon concept-building memories. For example, if a young child has had the experience of manipulating five blocks in various ways and is then encouraged visually to image the appearance of three small blocks and two small blocks making five blocks and auditorially to remember or image the sound of dropping three blocks and then two blocks into a metal pan, and to imagine the feel of letting the blocks drop, that child should have easy access to the memory.

Learning Styles and Exceptionality

In relating models of brain functioning to language development, human development, and environmental interactions, two basic features of young children's learning have been emphasized:

generativeness and individuality. How can teachers and parents apply these constructs in home and school? The emerging concept of learning styles offers substantial promise to respond to this question.

A child's learning style is the behavioral expression of an integrated cluster of features that make the child's approach to learning distinctive. These features, embedded in the deep structure of personality and development, give stylistic, consistent direction and depth to the child's learning behavior. The learning style accurately reflects the child's view of the world.

Bem and Allen (1974) proposed that there are a few stable characteristics that typify individual personality. The analogy of personality to learning style suggests that an operational definition of any child's learning style is the answer to the question "How do you know Dana or Juan or Becky or Steve as a distinctive person and thus as a learner?"

The child's learning style reflects a life-span development sequence; cognitive style changes over time.

Some approaches to learning styles are characterized by a heavy focus on manipulating specific external conditions of the learning environment and learning materials in response to preferences students indicate on questionnaires (Dunn and Dunn 1978). Fischer and Fischer (1979) state that such an approach, used alone, is naive and limited. The tendency to conceptualize individual differences in learning styles in narrow categories may cause us to lose the essence of the child's world view that really characterizes individual learning styles. Two different approaches are presented for the young child that can be appropriately applied to adults.

First, teachers and parents can focus on deeper features of individuality observable in children's behavior as well as children's orientation to and interpretation of learning experiences. For example, in what characteristic way do children seem to exhibit and employ the following features to create meaning and learn?

- orientation to and interest in certain classes of events, such as spatial constructive, verbal communicative, or emotionally weighted events
- sensitivity and responsiveness to people, animals, and inanimate materials
- sense of humor
- anxiety level
- tempo, including general level of arousal and energy, physical movement pattern, and pacing in learning tasks
- flexibility in degree and frequency of making adaptive shifts
- risk-taking or orientation to diverge from convention
- confidence in and acceptance of self as a personal causative agent within the sphere of direct experiences

Second, learning styles may be approached from a developmental perspective. One can expect the consistent and pervasive features defining the learning style of a child today to change over time under developmental influences. The child's learning style reflects a lifespan developmental sequence. The early childhood educator can look to developmental features to understand and predict changes in learning style. Bogen (1977) pointed out that attempts to equate right-left hemispheric brain functioning with models of cognitive style, such as field dependence-independence, are limited because cognitive style changes over time. Observed changes in learning style are associated with movement along the developmental life span, and the asssociated features emerge from psychological/biological/social roots.

Inheritance may be responsible for some organizational features of the brain and body. Such organization provides tendencies toward underlying learning styles that may or may not be fully expressed in the individual depending on the influence of environmental experiences. These experiences include pre- and postnatal nutrition and drug influences as well as family and cultural experiences. The release of hormones at certain points in development may serve as triggers for certain sensitive periods. The impact of these factors on individual learning styles is also influenced by the nature of environmental experiences. Those brain model programs that are established and those that are extinguished result from the interaction of the cluster of developmentally related influences.

The emerging concept of learning style also offers an approach to current trends in mainstreaming and exceptionality. In this country we have proceeded historically from a view excluding from the classroom those who were perceived as learning differently, including females, ethnic minorities, the mentally impaired, and the physically handicapped, to a more inclusive view reflected in mainstreaming legislation.

Throughout these changes, we have been plagued by the vicissitudes of labeling by which individuals are compartmentalized and their social movement constrained. Inherent in the plethora of terminology regarding exceptionality is a deficit view of life. Although designed to be helpful, many terms dealing with exceptionality carry what are actual or implied limiting or negative meanings. This is apparent for learning disabilities, but is also true for "gifted" learners. Current studies of brain functioning learning processes demonstrate that there are many ways to learn successfully. A genuine effort is needed to focus on the strengths of the differences rather than the limitations of the deficits.

Many of the labels for the exceptional learner not only induce negative biases but also cluster individuals inappropriately. For example, research reported by Knights and Bakker (1975) suggested that existing categories of learning disabilities do not effectively discriminate differences in learning. Instead, various neurological features of learning such as variation within a broad developmental profile, developmental lag, hemispheric asymmetry, perceptual anomalies, and sustained attention or focused arousal may represent useful building blocks for individual diagnosis and prescriptions for learning. Therefore we suggest viewing exceptionality in young learners from the proposed learning-styles model.

Suggested Readings

Dembo, M. H. *Teaching for Learning.* Santa Monica, Calif.: Goodyear, 1977.
Ernest, C. H. "Mental Imagery and Cognition: A Critical Review." *Journal of Mental Imagery* 1, no. 2 (1977): 181-217.

Jones, R. A. *Self-Fulfilling Prophecies: Social, Psychological, and Physiological Effects and Expectancies.* Hillsdale, N.J.: Lawrence Erlbaum Associates, 1977.

Joyce, B., and Weil, M. *Models of Teaching.* 2nd ed. Englewood Cliffs, N.J.: Prentice-Hall, 1979.

McGuigan, F. J., and Schoonover, R. A., eds. *The Psychophysiology of Thinking.* New York: Academic Press, 1973.

Pressley, M. "Imagery and Children's Learning: Putting the Picture in Developmental Perspective." *Review of Educational Research* 47, no. 4 (1977): 585-622.

Rentel, V., ed. *Psychobiological Aspects of Reading.* New York: Pergamon Press, forthcoming.

Wittrock, M. C. "The Cognitive Movement in Instruction." *Educational Psychologist* 13 (1978): 15-29.

III
Mobilizing for the Future

The acceptance of different ways of knowing (left and right hemisphere strategies) as legitimate methods of learning provides the first step toward building a balanced school program.

6
Mobilizing for Individuals

Three major areas for learning in young children have been considered from a theoretical perspective of brain functioning: (1) language development, (2) human development, and (3) environment and experience. Insights in brain functioning have the potential of exercising both a substantive and substantial influence on early childhood education in the years ahead. Policy and program implications project ways that professional leadership might capitalize on these understandings.

Policy Implications

Collaborate with Other Disciplines

The areas discussed in this book reflect an interdisciplinary perspective. Research for eventual classroom application develops when psychologists, linguists, anthropologists, neuroscientists, and educators pursue common issues. Such efforts hold promise of narrowing the gap between basic research and the classroom. Funding agencies consistently place priority on proposed activities built from interdisciplinary collaboration. The range of academic disciplines and professional roles represented by contributors to *Education and the Brain* (Chall and Mirsky 1978) further documents the interdisciplinary movement.

Accomplishing interdisciplinary collaboration is difficult. Active support of interdisciplinary efforts is an appropriate policy for national leaders in early childhood education. Examples of this policy might include—
1. sponsoring interdisciplinary activities at state, regional, and national meetings;
2. identifying people having common interests and activities and establishing interdisciplinary communication networks; and
3. promoting consortium-type efforts among professional organizations, child study centers, colleges and universities, and federal and state agencies.

Reach Decision Makers

The emerging notions treated in this book and other futuristic ideas must be brought to the attention of people with decision-making and resource allocation responsibilities. A direct expression would be the presentation of such ideas at meetings of funding and leadership agencies where decisions are made about support and development priorities. An indirect effort would be supporting individuals for policy positions who have the needed vision of future professional and political commitment to children, families, and education.

Increase Awareness

Active promotion and dissemination of documents delineating future directions in early childhood education are needed to increase awareness, development, involvement, and eventual application of emerging conceptions. For example, early childhood educators should support the services of the ERIC Clearinghouse on Elementary and Early Childhood Education (ERIC/EECE) and professional journals and publications of such organizations as the National Association for the Education of Young Children (NAEYC) and the Society for Research in Child Development (SRCD).

Provide Organizational Leadership

Within the early childhood professional community, organizations such as the National Association for the Education of Young Children have a leadership responsibility to establish and develop future directions for the early childhood community. This can be done through professional meetings and publications, through coordination with allied organizations, and through support of policy decisions and interdisciplinary efforts to continue to improve early childhood education.

Program Implications

The acceptance of different ways of knowing (left and right hemisphere strategies) as legitimate methods of learning provides the first step toward building a balanced school program. At present, our lopsided educational system emphasizes narrowly defined linear skills and leaves half of the child's learning capacities unschooled. Complete understanding in learning comes from integrating both ways of knowing. Thus, the educational program can be compatible with the brain. The brain organizes its various functions to provide the individual with a single, integrated stream of consciousness. If our brain's orientation is "to get it all together," surely our schooling should do no less.

Curricular development might be approached through the interaction model of hemispheric processing. For example, in children's literature, both abilities are valued in the unity of illustrations (visuo-spatial) with the text (verbal). Moffett supported the integration of hemispheric modalities in discussing the role of the metaphor in literature and content fields (Sohn 1975). Effective and responsible use of media and children's television programming is needed. Instructional aspects of curriculum clearly relate to the research of Paivio (1971, 1973) and Wittrock (1977, 1978b) in using imagery in instruction.

The motoric base of learning may help us better understand the value of hands-on curriculum experiences. Two consistent research findings in science education research literature seem to support this idea. First, in classrooms using the contemporary hands-on science curriculum, the concept achievement of inner-city students, characteristically much lower in verbal educational performance, approximates that of their suburban peers (Walbesser 1968). Second, there is a marked increase in students' language skills associated with using these curriculums (Huff and Languis 1973). Wittrock (1977) has suggested that adults first assess the child's learning preference; then directly challenge the individual's preferred mode and supplement this instruction to encourage the other hemisphere to participate.

Integration of the brain's two thinking systems has also been suggested as a model of creativity. Bogen and Bogen (1969) proposed that creative productivity involves both the intuitive sensing of patterns and the analytic organization of ideas into propositions, thus tapping the high-level cognitive capabilities of both hemispheres. Moreover, they suggest that access to and communication between the hemispheres may be the key to expanding creative potential. Therefore, an appropriate program goal might be to facilitate in children the ability to shift flexibly between both modes of thinking and to use, value, and trust ideas derived equally from both strategies.

The research and teaching of Edwards (1979) provides an illustration: She found that when she asked beginning level college students to view an upside-down Picasso sketch and draw it upside down, rather than in the usual upright manner, their performance markedly improved. She inferred that drawing upside down, by reducing the logicalness of the task, caused the left hemisphere to release its control. With this slight shift in consciousness, the right hemisphere was able to bring its spatial expertise to bear on the drawing task. Once this ability to shift was comfortably attained, the students could use both spatial holistic and analytic techniques in building overall drawing competence.

Value Differences

Geschwind focused upon the values assigned to certain learning abilities when he commented—

> One must remember that practically all of us have a significant number of learning disabilities . . . we happen to live in a society where the child who has trouble learning to read is in difficulty. Yet we have all seen some dyslexic children who draw much better than "normal" children, i.e., who have either superior visual perception or visual motor skills. (1975, p. 193)

In another setting these children might excel. As the demands of our society change, we may label a different group of people "disabled," but a more productive approach would be to value the differences rather than decry the deficits. Guyer and Friedman (1975) found that learning-disabled children were not deficient in right hemisphere skills, nor were they deficient in all aspects of verbal ability when compared with normal children. They seemed to be attempting to use a nonverbal modality to solve academic tasks.

Verbal skills in reading and writing provide passports to success in American schools today. The lack of success we have with many children, especially low socioeconomic status children and boys (approximately a four-to-one ratio over girls in remedial reading classes), suggests that we need to use knowledge about nonlinear representational systems to develop more appropriate school programs for children who, because of differences in learning styles, developmental lag, etc., learn differently (Languis and Kraft, forthcoming).

Brain research also indicates developmental differences. Harris (1976) proposed developmental changes in cognitive style associated with brain functioning models. Restructuring and developing more adequate models of cognitive or learning styles to better explain individual differences seems warranted. Berlin (1978) found support for an association between hemispheric brain lateralization and development of field dependence-independence cognitive styles, especially for boys.

Create a Supportive Classroom Atmosphere

Emotion has often been assigned to the "warm fuzzy" thinking of humanists while rationality has been associated with a cognitive orientation. Effective teachers have always known that isolating emotions from cognition in young children's learning is nonsense. The generative and interactive physiopsychosocial view of learning we have emphasized provides an integrative model for program development. The role of the limbic system in control of emotion in learning confounds its crucial role in relaying information to the neocortex. Emotion contributes the color, vitality, and motivational components of learning. In contrast, Tobias (1978) found that anxiety changes processing mechanisms, coding processes, and memory function. This research supports Hart's (1978) hypothesis that under distress the brain downshifts to older structures. Therefore, under

Isolating emotions from cognition in young children's learning is nonsense.

distress or threat, a flight-fight response is elicited instead of the neocortex being able to learn or weigh alternative decisions. Because neither a flight nor a fight response is usually acceptable in social settings, the frustration builds internally and over time may lead to the stress-related disorders that are prevalent in all age groups in contemporary American culture. Parents, teachers, and children recognize that how to cope with stress is an area of major concern in education. Individuals vary widely in their response to stressors, but teachers should provide young children with a supportive non-threatening classroom atmosphere for optimal learning.

Establish Life Control

Life control is a basic component that underlies concerns about schooling practices. How strongly do our children believe in themselves as sources of influence and responsibility for what happens? In the socialization process of the home, school, and society, children gradually build a personal view of life control. Rowe (1978) expressed this idea as a "craps vs. bowlers" view of control over fate.

DeCharms (1976) demonstrated academic achievement gains in high school students by teaching teachers to teach students to believe in themselves as origins rather than as pawns. The program worked better for boys than girls. Wolfe (1976) used temperature training biofeedback with an experimental group of her inner-city kindergarten children to help them gain confidence in their ability to control their own bodies. She found that the internal locus of control was improved at post-test and at a six week delayed post-test in comparison with locus-of-control assessment of her placebo and control-group students. Wittrock (1978a) suggested that the level of students' realistic belief in personal causation and individual responsibility is a powerful force in instructional settings and, moreover, that it results from an active process by which children build their perspective of their control over fate.

Brain functioning research and the generative view of the learning process in young children provide useful approaches for dealing positively with personal causation.

> If learning is believed to be an internally mediated process that the learners can influence through their effort and hard work, the consequences for the students go beyond the mastery of subject matter to include possibly the development of a sense of self-control over one's destiny and a sense of personal responsibility for one's behavior. To paraphrase Robert Hutchins, the problem with reinforcement theory is not that it is wrong, but that it might come true; that is, the learners might start to believe that the world controls them rather than that they can control it. (Wittrock 1978a, p. 20)

Perhaps the life-control view just suggested will help mobilize early childhood leaders as they attempt to make futuristic ideas present realities. By their career focus, people involved in various aspects of early childhood education programs—teacher education, research and theory, professional leadership—already have a futuristic orientation. We are a large and strong professional force. With realism and optimism, we suggest placing new threads on the loom to establish future directions for early childhood education.

References

Albert, M. L., and Obler, L. K. *The Bilingual Brain.* New York: Academic Press, 1978.

Allwood, C. M. "A Review of Individual Differences among Problem Solvers and Attempts to Improve Problem Solving Ability." *Psychological Reports* (University of Goteborg, Sweden) 6 (1976): 1-27.

Baltes, P., and Willis, L. "Life Span Developmental Psychology, Cognitive Functioning and Social Policy." In *Aging from Birth to Death,* ed. M. W. Riley. AAS Selected Symposium, No. 30. Washington, D.C.: American Association for the Advancement of Science, 1979.

Bates, E. *Language and Context: The Acquisition of Pragmatics.* New York: Academic Press, 1976.

Bem, D. J., and Allen, A. "Predicting Some of the People Some of the Time: The Search for Cross-Situational Consistencies in Behavior." *Psychological Review* 81 (1974): 506-520.

Berlin, D. "The Relationship Between a Developmental Theory of Hemispheric Brain Lateralization and Age and Sex Differences in Field Dependence-Independence and Visuo-Spatial Measures." Doctoral dissertation, The Ohio State University, 1978.

Bloom, L. *One Word at a Time: The Use of Single Word Utterances Before Syntax.* The Hague: Mouton, 1973.

Bogen, J. E. "Educational Aspects and Hemispheric Specialization." In *The Human Brain,* ed. M. C. Wittrock. Englewood Cliffs, N.J.: Prentice-Hall, 1977.

Bogen, J. E., and Bogen, G. M. "The Other Side of the Brain III: The Corpus Callosum and Creativity." *Bulletin of Los Angeles Neurological Society* 34 (1969): 191-220.

Britton, J. *Language and Learning.* Harmonsworth, England: Penguin, 1970.

Bruner, J. "The Ontogenesis of Speech Acts." *Journal of Child Language* 2, no. 2 (1975): 1-19.

Buck, R. *Human Motivation and Behavior.* New York: Wiley, 1976.

Carter, A. "The Transformation of Sensory Motor Morphemes into Words." In *Papers and Reports of Child Language Development,* No. 10, ed. E. Clark. Palo Alto, Calif.: Stanford University, 1975.

Cazden, C. "Suggestions from Studies of Early Language Acquisition." In *Language and the Language Arts,* ed. J. DeStefano and S. E. Fox. Boston: Little, Brown, 1974.

Chall, J. S., and Mirsky, A. F. *Education and the Brain.* 77th National Society for the Study of Education Yearbook, Park II. Chicago: University of Chicago Press, 1978.

Clay, M. M. *What Did I Write?* New York: International Publications Service, 1975.

Cook-Gumperz, J., and Gumperz, J. J. "Context in Children's Speech." In *The Development of Communication,* ed. V. Waterson and C. Snow. New York: Wiley, 1978.

Corrigan, R. "The Relationship Between Object Permanence and Language Development: How Much and How Strong?" Paper presented at Stanford Child Language Research Forum, Stanford University, Palo Alto, Calif., April 1976.

Cunningham, R. T. "Questioning Behavior, or, How Are You at P. R.?" In *Implementing Teacher Competencies,* ed. J. E. Weigand. Englewood Cliffs, N.J.: Prentice-Hall, 1977.

DeCharms, R. *Enhancing Motivation: Change in the Classroom.* New York: Halsted Press, 1976.

DeStefano, J. *Language, the Learner, and the School.* New York: Wiley, 1978.

Dewing, K., and Hetherington, P. "Anagram Solving as a Function of Word Imagery." *Journal of Experimental Psychology* 102 (1974): 764-767.

Dihoff, R., and Chapman, R. "First Words: Their Origin in Action." In *Papers and Reports of Child Language Development,* No. 13, ed. E. Clark. Palo Alto, Calif.: Stanford University, 1977.

Dunn, R., and Dunn, K. *Teaching Students Through Their Individual Learning Styles: A Practical Approach.* Reston, Va.: Reston Publishing Co., 1978.

Edwards, B. *Drawing on the Right Side of the Brain.* Los Angeles: J. P. Tarcher, 1979.

Epstein, H. T. "Growth Spurts During Brain Development: Implications for Educational Policy and Practice." In *Education and the Brain,* 77th National Society for the Study of Education Yearbook, ed. J. Chall and A. F. Mirsky. Chicago: University of Chicago Press, 1978.

Ernest, C. H. "Mental Imagery and Cognition: A Critical Review." *Journal of Mental Imagery* 1, no. 2 (1977): 181-217.

Ernest, C. H., and Paivio, A. "Imagery and Verbal Associative Latercies as a Function of Imagery Ability." *Canadian Journal of Psychology* 25 (1971): 83-90.

Fischer, B. B., and Fischer, L. "Styles in Teaching and Learning." *Educational Leadership* 36, no. 4 (1979): 245-254.

Flaherty, E. G. "The Thinking Aloud Technique and Problem Solving Ability." *Journal of Educational Research* 68 (1975): 223-225.
Fuller, F. F., and Bowen, O. H. "Becoming a Teacher." In *Teacher Education*, 74th National Society for the Study of Education Yearbook, Part II, ed. K. Ryan. Chicago: University of Chicago Press, 1975.
Galin, D.; Johnstone, J.; Nakell, L.; and Herron, J. "Development of the Capacity for Tactile Information Transfer Between Hemispheres in Normal Children." *Science* 204 (1979): 1330-1331.
Galin, D., and Ornstein, R. E. "Hemispheric Specialization and the Duality of Consciousness." In *Human Behavior and Brain Function*, ed. W. J. Widroe. Springfield, Ill.: Charles C. Thomas, 1975.
Geschwind, N. "The Apraxias: Neural Mechanisms of Disorders of Learned Movement." *American Scientist* 63 (1975): 188-195.
Glickman, C., and Christie, D. "The Effects of Classroom Noise on Children: Evidence of Sex Differences." *Psychology in the Schools*, in press.
Goodman, M. E. *The Culture of Childhood*. New York: Teachers College Press, Columbia University, 1971.
Gould, R. *Transformation: Growth and Change in Adult Life*. New York: Simon & Schuster, 1978.
Graves, D. H. "Balance the Basics, Let them Write." *Ford Foundation Reports*, ed. R. Magat. New York: Ford Foundation Office of Reports, 1978.
Greenfield, P., and Smith, J. *The Structure of Communication in Early Language Development*. New York: Academic Press, 1976.
Guyer, B. L., and Friedman, M. P. "Hemispheric Processing and Cognitive Styles in Learning Disabled and Normal Children." *Child Development* 46 (1975): 658-668.
Harding, C., and Golingkoff, R. "The Relationship Between Early Language Research and Cognitive Development." Paper presented at The Society for Research in Child Development, Denver, Colo., March 1977.
Harnad, S.; Doty, R. W.; Goldstein, L.; Jayles, J.; and Krauthamer, G. *Lateralization in the Nervous System*. New York: Academic Press, 1977.
Harris, L. J. "Sex Differences in Spatial Ability: Possible Environmental Genetic and Neurological Factors." In *Hemispheric Asymmetries of Function*, ed. M. Kinsbourne. Cambridge: Cambridge University Press, 1976.
Hart, L. A. *How the Brain Works*. New York: Basic Books, 1975.
Hart, L. A. "The New Brain Concept of Learning." *Phi Delta Kappan* 59 (1978): 393-396.
Hebb, D. O. *The Organization of Behavior*. New York: Wiley, 1949.

Hebb, D. O. "Watching Myself Get Old." *Psychology Today* 2, no. 8 (November 1978): 15.

Huff, P., and Languis, M. L. "The Effects of the Use of Activities of SAPA on the Oral Communication Skills of Disadvantaged Kindergarten Children." *Journal of Research in Science Teaching* 10 (1973): 165-173.

Hunt, J. M. "Psychological Development: Early Experience." *Annual Review of Psychology* 30 (1979): 103-143.

Ingram, D. "Sensorimotor Intelligence and Language Development." In *Action, Gesture, and Symbol: The Emergence of Language*, ed. A. Lock. New York: Academic Press, 1976.

Jerison, H. J. "Evolution of the Brain." In *The Human Brain*, ed. M. C. Wittrock. Englewood Cliffs, N.J.: Prentice-Hall, 1977.

Katz, L. G. *Talks with Teachers*. Washington, D.C.: National Association for the Education of Young Children, 1977.

Kimura, D. "Cerebral Dominance and the Perception of Verbal Stimuli." *Canadian Journal of Psychology* 15 (1961): 166-171.

Kimura, D. "Dual Functioning Asymmetry of the Brain in Visual Perception." *Neuropsychologia* 4 (1966): 275-286.

Kinsbourne, M. "Evolution of Language in Relation to Lateral Action." In *Asymmetrical Function of the Brain*, ed. M. Kinsbourne. Cambridge: Cambridge University Press, 1978.

Klima, E. S. "How Alphabets Might Reflect Language." In *Language by Ear and by Eye*, ed. I. Mattingly and J. Kavanaugh. Cambridge, Mass.: MIT Press, 1972.

Knights, R. M., and Bakker, D. J. *The Neuropsychology of Learning Disorders*. Baltimore: University Park Press, 1975.

Knox, C., and Kimura, D. "Cerebral Processing of Nonverbal Sounds in Boys and Girls." *Neuropsychologia* 8 (1970): 227-237.

Kosslyn, S. "Imagery and Cognitive Development: A Teleological Approach." In *Children's Thinking: What Develops*, ed. R. S. Siegler. Hillsdale, N.J.: Lawrence Erlbaum Associates, 1978.

Kraft, R. H. "An EEG Study: Hemispheric Brain Functioning of Six to Eight Year Old Children during Piagetian and Curriculum Tasks with Variation in Presentation Mode." Doctoral dissertation, The Ohio State University, 1976.

Kraft, R. H., and Languis, M. L. "Dimensions of Right and Left Brain Learning." In *Early Childhood Education*, ed. L. H. Golubchick and B. Perskey. New York: Avery Press, 1977.

Kraft, R. H. "Asymmetric Brain Specialization Proposed Relationship Between Its Development and Cognitive Development." In *Psychological Aspects of Reading*, ed. V. Rentel. New York: Pergamon, in press.

Krashen, S. D. "The Left Hemisphere." In *The Human Brain*, ed. M. C. Wittrock. Englewood Cliffs, N.J.: Prentice-Hall, 1977.

Languis, M. L., and Kraft, R. "Hemispheric Brain Function—What It Means for You." *OCESS Journal* 7, no. 2 (1976): 14-18.

Languis, M. L., and Kraft, R. "An Educational Perspective on the Hemispheric Process of the Brain." Urbana, Ill.: University of Illinois, 1978. ERIC Document No. ED 151748.

Languis, M. L., and Kraft, R. H. "A Conceptual Overview of the Hemispheric Process of the Brain." In *Psychological Aspects of Reading*, ed. V. Rentel. New York: Pergamon, forthcoming.

Lashley, K. S. "The Mechanism of Vision: XII. Nervous Structures Concerned in Habits Based on Reaction to Light." *Comparative Psychology Monographs* 11 (1935): 43-79.

Lefcourt, H. M. *Locus of Control: Current Trends in Theory and Research*. New York: Halsted Press, 1976.

Leiderman, P. H. "The Critical Period Hypotheses Revisited: Mother to Infant Bonding in the Neonatal Period." In *Early Developmental Hazards: Predictors and Precautions*, ed. F. D. Horowitz. AAAS Selected Symposium, No. 19. Washington, D.C.: American Association for the Advancement of Science, 1978.

Levinson, D. J. *The Seasons of Man's Life*. New York: Knopf, 1978.

Levy, J.; Trevarthen, C.; and Sperry, R. W. "Perception of Bilateral Chimeric Figures Following Hemispheric Deconnection." *Cortex* 95 (1972): 61-68.

Lezine, I. "The Transition from Sensorimotor to Earliest Symbolic Function in Early Development." In *Early Development*, No. 149. Chicago: University of Chicago Press, 1973.

Loevinger, J. *Ego Development*. San Francisco: Jossey-Bass, 1976.

Lowenthal, M. F.; Thurnhe, M.; and Chiriboga, D. C. *Four Stages of Life: A Comparative Study of Women and Men Facing Transitions*. New York: Jossey-Bass, 1975.

Luria, A. R. *The Working Brain*. New York: Penguin, 1973.

McGuiness, D., and Pribram, K. H. "The Origins of Sensory Bias in the Development of Gender Differences in Perception and Cognition." In *Cognitive Growth and Development: Essays in Memory of Herbert G. Birch*, ed. M. Bortner. New York: Brunner/Mazel, 1978.

MacLean, P. D. "A Mind of Three Minds: Educating the Triune Brain." In *Education and the Brain*, 77th National Society for the Study of Education Yearbook, ed. J. Chall and A. F. Mirsky. Chicago: University of Chicago Press, 1978.

Maslow, A. H. *Motivation and Personality*. New York: Harper & Row, 1954.

Mattingly, I. G., and Kavanaugh, J. F. *Language by Ear and by Eye: The Relationships Between Speech and Reading.* Cambridge, Mass.: MIT Press, 1972.

Meyer, D. R., and Meyer, P. M. "Induction of Recovery from Amnesia." In *Learning and Memory,* ed. J. L. McGaugh and R. F. Thompson. New York: Plenum, forthcoming.

Paivio, A. *Imagery and Verbal Process.* New York: Holt, Rinehart & Winston, 1971.

Paivio, A. "Psychophysiological Correlates of Imagery." In *The Psychophysiology of Thinking,* ed. F. J. McGuigan and R. A. Schounover. New York: Academic Press, 1973.

Perkes, V. A. "Tyranny of Words." *Science and Children* 9, no. 1 (September 1971): 17-18.

Pressley, M. "Imagery and Children's Learning: Putting the Picture in Developmental Perspective." *Review of Educational Research* 47, no. 4 (1977): 585-622.

Pribram, K. H. *Language of the Brain.* Englewood Cliffs, N.J.: Prentice-Hall, 1971.

Raph, J., and Nicholich, L. "Symbolic Play and the Development of Language." Paper presented at the American Psychological Association Meeting, Chicago, Ill., 1975.

Read, C. "Children's Categorization of Speech Sounds in English." Research Report No. 17. Urbana, Ill.: National Council of Teachers of English, 1975.

Restak, R. M. *The Brain: The Last Frontier.* Garden City, N.Y.: Doubleday, 1979.

Riegel, K. R. "Toward a Dialectical Theory of Development." *Human Development* 18 (1975): 50-64.

Rice, D. R., and Languis, M. L. "What Is for Real in Communication: Your Right-Left Brain Decides." *Reading Improvement* 1 (Spring 1979): 50-54.

Rowe, M. B. *Teaching Science Is Continuous Inquiry.* New York: McGraw-Hill, 1978.

Sagan, C. *The Dragons of Eden.* New York: Ballantine, 1977.

Sandman, C. A., and Kastin, A. J. "Neuropeptide Influences on Behavior: A Possible Treatment for Disorders of Attention," pp. 287-295. In *Neuroregulation and Hypotheses Concerning Psychiatric Disorders,* ed. J. Barchas, D. Hamburg, and E. Usdin. Oxford: Oxford University Press, 1977.

Seamon, J., and Gazzaniga, A. "Coding Strategies and Cerebral Laterality Effects." *Cognitive Psychology* 5 (1973): 249-254.

Searlman, A. "A Review of Right Hemisphere Linguistic Capabilities." *Psychological Bulletin* 84 (1977): 503-522.

Sheehan, P. W. "A Functional Analysis of the Role of Visual Imagery in Unexpected Recall." In *The Function and Nature of Imagery*, ed. P. Sheehan. New York: Academic Press, 1972.
Smilansky, S. *The Effects of Sociodramatic Play on Disadvantaged Pre-School Children*. New York: Wiley, 1968.
Sohn, D. "A Talk with James Moffett." *Media and Methods* 14 (1975): 2-6.
Sperry, R. W.; Gazzaniga, M. S.; and Bogen, J. E. "Interhemispheric Relationships, the Neocortical Commissures: Syndromes of Hemispheric Disconnection." In *Handbook of Clinical Neurology*, Vol. IV. Amsterdam: Elsevier-North Holland Publishing Co., 1969.
Stellar, E.; Sprague, J. M.; and Chambers, W. W. "Control of Posture by Reticular Formation and Cerebellum in Intact Anesthetized and in Anesthetized De-Cerebrated Cats." *American Journal of Physiology* 176 (1954): 52-64.
Stratton, R. P.; Jacobus, K. A.; and Leonard, S. D. "Solving Anagrams as a Function of Word Frequency, Imagery, and Distribution of Practice." *Canadian Journal of Psychology* 76 (1970): 279-287.
Thompson, R. F. *Introduction to Physiological Psychology*. New York: Harper & Row, 1975.
Tobias, S. *Overcoming Math Anxiety*. New York: Norton, 1978.
Walbesser, H. H., ed. "An Evaluation Model and Its Application." Second Report, Commission on Science Education, American Association for the Advancement of Science, Washington, D.C., 1968.
Walker, J. A. "Developing Efficacy, Sense of Efficacy, and Self-Esteem Through Training." Doctoral dissertation, The University of Michigan, 1970.
White, S. H., and Siegel, A. W. "Cognitive Development: The New Inquiry." *Young Children* 31, no. 6 (1976): 425-436.
Williams, C. R. "In the Beginning—Goals." *Theory Into Practice* 15, no. 2 (April 1976): 86-89.
Williams, F.; Hopper, R.; Natalicio, P. *The Sounds of Children*. Englewood Cliffs, N.J.: Prentice-Hall, 1977.
Winick, M. *Malnutrition and Brain Development*. Oxford: Oxford University Press, 1976.
Witelson, S. F. "Developmental Dyslexia: Two Right Hemispheres and None Left." *Science* 195 (1977): 309-311.
Wittrock, M. C. *The Human Brain*. Englewood Cliffs, N.J.: Prentice-Hall, 1977.
Wittrock, M. C. "The Cognitive Movement in Instruction." *Educational Psychologist* 13 (1978a): 15-29.

Wittrock. M. C. "Education and the Cognitive Process of the Brain." In *Education and the Brain*, 77th National Society for the Study of Education Yearbook. Part II, ed. J. Chall and A. F. Mirsky. Chicago: University of Chicago Press, 1978b.

Wolfe, B. L. "The Effect of Biofeedback Experience upon Change in Locus of Control of Disadvantaged Kindergarten Children." Masters thesis, The Ohio State University, 1976.

Wolfgang, C. H. *Helping Aggressive and Passive Preschool Children Through Play.* Columbus, Ohio: Merrill, 1977.

Wood, D.; Shotter, J.; and Godden, D. "An Investigation of the Relationships Between Problem Solving Strategies, Representation and Memory." *Quarterly Journal of Experimental Psychology* 26 (1974): 252-257.

Yarrow, M. R., and Waxler, L. J. *Infant and Environment: Early Cognitive and Motivational Development.* New York: Halsted Press, 1975.

Young, J. Z. *Programs of the Brain.* Oxford: Oxford University Press, 1978.

Glossary of Terms

Afferent nerves. The fibers which carry sensory input from skin, muscles, joints, deep tissues, and other sense receptors toward the cortex and other portions of the central nervous system.

Amygdala. One of the interconnected structures of the limbic system the function of which has been proposed to be related to emotional experience and releasing natural pain-suppressing substances called endorphins.

Axon. The major type of communicating link between neurons. Axons are long and slender and carry (conduct) electrical impulses away from the cell body of one neuron to some portion of another neuron. Also known as nerve fiber, clusters or bundles of axons form nerves.

Brain stem. The lower portion of the brain consisting of the midbrain, pons, and medulla. This region of the central nervous system includes, among other structures, (1) tracts carrying sensory information from skin, muscles, joints, cornea, ears, and mouth to forebrain areas, notably the thalamus; (2) axon bundles conveying motor commands from the cerebral cortex to motor centers in the brain stem and spinal cord; (3) raphe nuclei (implicated in regulation of sleep cycles); (4) reticular formation (critical in the control of arousal, focusing attention and gross bodily muscle tone); and (5) cardiac and respiratory centers.

Broca's area. An area in the human frontal cortex of the left hemisphere that has been closely related to both syntatic and phonemic aspects of language function and to language production.

Cerebellum. A large, highly convoluted structure immediately behind the brain stem (see brain diagram, p. 7) with which it is intimately connected. The cerebellum appears to play an important role in maintaining postural symmetry between right and left halves of the body and in timing and coordinating movements.

Cerebral cortex. Multilayered tissue forming the outer surface of the forebrain. A portion of this tissue, specifically the neocortex, has undergone the greatest proportional increase in the evolution of the mammalian brain. The neocortex is believed to be critically involved in higher cognitive functions.

Cerebral hemisphere. The outermost portion of the forebrain, consisting essentially of what is called the telencephalon (cerebral cortex, corpus callosum, basal ganglia, and limbic system). Because the various parts of the telencephalon, which together comprise an appreciable portion of the forebrain, are each found clearly separated from one another on both right and left sides of the brain, each half (right and left) of the telencephalon is called a cerebral hemisphere.

Contralateral. Opposite side or crossed; for example, auditory connections between the right ear and left hemisphere and left ear and right hemisphere are *contralateral* connections.

Corpus callosum. A massive commissure connecting the right and left cerebral hemispheres (see brain diagram, p. 7). Axons leading from neurons in half of the cerebral cortex (e.g. right) always terminate in the corresponding area of the other hemisphere (e.g. left). The corpus callosum thus allows the two halves of the cerebral cortex to communicate directly with one another.

Dendrites. Receptive extensions of a cell body that receive input from other cell bodies. Dendrites are characteristically bush-like or branching in appearance.

Dendritic branching. Bush-like extensions of a neuron or nerve cell that functionally connect the cell to input from numerous other cells.

Dichaptic technique. A procedure for simultaneously presenting competing tactile stimuli to both hemispheres.

Dichotic technique. A procedure for simultaneously presenting competing stimuli, usually auditory, to both hemispheres.

Dyslexia. A central nervous system disorder in which the comprehension of written language (i.e. reading) is impaired.

Efferent nerves. The fibers which carry impulses away from cell bodies in the cortex or other portions of the central nervous system, resulting in motor innervation or movement.

Electroencephalogram (EEG). The pattern of electrical activity that may be recorded from the cerebral cortex using electrodes placed on the surface of the scalp.

Endocrine (ductless) gland. Non-neural secretory tissue which, unlike exocrine or ducted glands, uses blood vessels and perhaps the lymph system to carry its secretions (hormones) to their target area of action. Among these are the pituitary, thyroid, and adrenal glands. Via their hormonal output, endocrine glands affect the central nervous system; via hypothalamic control of the pituitary gland, the central nervous system affects the endocrine glands.

Engram. A hypothesized concept for the physical basis of memory; a memory trace. A neurological artifact of learning; the set of physical processes and changes in the brain that form the basis of something learned.

Forebrain (prosencephalon). The highest and most prominent portion of the brain which has undergone the greatest evolutionary expansion of any nervous system region. The major subdivisions of the forebrain are (1) the cerebral cortex (critically involved in cognitive functions), (2) the basal ganglia (motor system modulator), (3) the limbic system (subserving emotional and sexual behavior as well as implicated in mediation of memory processes), (4) the thalamus (relaying sensory, motor, and limbic information to the cerebral cortex and basal ganglia), and (5) the hypothalamus (critically involved in the control or modulation of numerous basic behaviors such as eating, drinking, sleeping, sexual activity, aggression, etc. as well as bodily temperature and hormone regulation).

Frontal lobe. The area of the cerebral cortex toward the front of the head (see brain diagram, p. 7) encased in large part by the forehead and temples.

Gating function. The role played by the Reticular Activating System and other neuronal networks in selectively transmitting stimuli higher and lower in the central nervous system.

Generative processing. In learning, cognitive processing that involves the active construction of meaning for stimuli by the individual.

Glia. A type of cell found in the nervous system which far outnumbers neurons. These cells do not generate spikes or impulses as do neurons but may play a role in myelinating axons, guiding the regrowth of damaged axons in some parts of the nervous system, and perhaps regulating neurotransmitter storage and release. Glia may also play a role in maintaining the blood-brain barrier.

Hippocampus. A part of the limbic system named for its resemblance to a sea horse;

the function of the hippocampus has been proposed to be related to aspects of memory, cognitive mapping, and response to novelty in the environment.

Holistic. With reference to cognitive functions, the simultaneous processing of a configuration of information, rather than the sequential processing of its separate parts.

Homeostasis. In physiology, a steady, optimal state of the body by which an organism maintains through feedback controlled biological activities known as homeostatic processes.

Hypothalamus. A portion of the diencephalon or midbrain which is structurally and functionally complex. Though a relatively small part of the brain, the hypothalamus is comprised of nuclei with widespread connections to and from other parts of the brain including frontal lobes and brain stem structure.

Ipsilateral. Same-sided or uncrossed; for example, the anatomical connections between the cerebellum and motor pathways are such that each hemisphere of the cerebellum is related to motor activity on the ipsilateral same side of the body.

Lateralization (hemispheric). The differentiation of the two cerebral hemispheres with respect to function.

Lesion. As a verb, lesion is the process of damaging bodily tissue by cutting, heating, applying toxic substances, etc. As a noun, lesion refers to the focal area of tissue damage.

Limbic system. An interconnected set of forebrain structures including the amygdala, septum, hippocampus, and the cingulate cortex. The system both receives input from, and directs output to, the thalamus, hypothalamus, and brain stem. Similar to the hypothalamus, limbic system structures modulate motivational (e.g. eating and drinking), emotional (e.g. aggression), and sexual behavior. In addition, the hippocampus has been implicated in memory mechanisms.

Lobes of cerebral cortex. The major structural divisions of the cerebral cortex visible to the naked eye, differentiated primarily by prominent cerebral convolutions. These consist of the frontal, parietal, occipital, temporal, and limbic lobes (see brain diagram, p. 7).

Myelin sheath. The fatty substance partially covering some axons. Myelin serves to increase the speed with which impulses travel along nerve fibers.

Myelination. The development of an insulating sheath surrounding large nerve fibers. Myelination facilitates transmission of impulses along the fibers.

Neocortex. Literally, *new brain*; a term used to refer to the cerebral cortex as the most recent evolutionary development of the vertebrate nervous system.

Neuron. A nerve cell body and its connections; the basic functional unit of the nervous system. The nervous system is composed largely of neurons and another type of cell known as *glia*.

Neuroscience. The multidisciplinary study of the structure, chemical composition, and function (biological and behavioral) of the nervous system.

Neurotransmitter. A chemical substance released across the synaptic gap to influence the electrical activity of the receiving neuron. Often abbreviated *transmitter*.

Nucleus. In neuroanatomy, collections of nerve cell bodies within areas or structures of the central nervous system.

Occipital lobe. The part of the cerebral cortex directly behind the parietal and temporal lobes (see brain diagram, p. 7) and adjacent to the skull along the lower back portion of the head. This region consists largely of the area of the cerebral cortex most directly in receipt of visual (light) information.

Olfactory. Pertaining to the sense of smell.

Ontogeny. Refers to the growth and development of an individual organism as opposed to the evolutionary development of a species.

Parietal lobe. The cerebral cortical lobe directly behind the frontal lobe and immediately above the posterior end of the temporal lobe (see brain diagram, p. 7). This region contains the area of the cerebral cortex most directly in receipt of sensory information from the skin and muscles: touch, pressure, position sense, etc.

Peptides. A class of biochemical substances comprised of bonded protein chains. Peptides are believed to influence the function of the nervous system and the transmission of impulses at the synapses as do neurotransmitters.

Phrenology. An early theory of localized brain function which proposed determination of specific character traits on the basis of superficial properties of the skull.

Phylogeny. The evolutionary history of a species as opposed to the growth of a single organism (ontogeny) with which it is often contrasted.

Pituitary gland. The master gland controlling the release of hormones from other endocrine glands. Located just beneath the hypothalamus, with which it is connected via neural and vascular tissue, the pituitary gland is controlled by this brain structure and hormones released by other endocrine glands. Because the hypothalamus is also influenced by those hormones, the pituitary is to a large extent regulated by direct and indirect feedback systems, both of which are inhibitory in nature.

Prosters. Leslie Hart's term for established internalized categories of experience and expectations.

Reticular Activating System. A functional reticulum or network of nuclei in the brain stem and their connective ascending sensory and descending motor pathways. This system plays a role in general levels of attention, arousal, sleep, and integration of brain activity.

Substrates. Underlying structures, foundations, or necessary preexisting elements.

Sulcus (pl. sulci). A distinct infolding or groove in the surface of the cerebral cortex. Especially prominent sulci are called fissures (e.g. Sylvian fissure). The large number and complicated patterns of sulci are an obvious distinguishing feature of cetacean and primate brains.

Synapse. The point of electrical or chemical interaction and contact between two neurons or between a neuron and a muscle fiber or neurosecretory cell; often used synonymously with synaptic gap.

Synaptic gap. A very small space between the two contacting surfaces, such as the cleft between the axon terminal of one neuron and the dendrite or cell body of another neuron.

Tactual (tactile). The sense of touch, one of a number of somatic (body) sensations.

Temporal lobe. The lowest-lying lobe of the cerebral cortex located below the frontal and parietal lobes and adjacent to that portion of the skull just above the ears. This area of the cerebral cortex receives auditory information.

Thalamus. A complex group of nuclei in the midbrain with projections up to the cortex and limbic system and down to lower brain regions as well. Functionally, these nuclei are involved in relay of incoming sensory information to the cortex and other processes not yet fully understood.

Wernicke's area. An area in the left cerebral hemisphere near the border between the temporal and parietal lobes which is crucial to language comprehension.

Index

activity 19
  beta wave 30
  brain 14
  interdisciplinary 47
  language 21
  left- and right-brain 12
adult
  brain 38
  -child communication 36
  -child developmental lines 27
  development 28
  listener 22
  performance model 35
  role of, 21
  speech 20
altruism 30
amygdala 6
anxiety level 41
apathy 38
aphasia 32
auditory input 12
axons 6

behavior 13, 14
  children's 41
  human 15, 16
  learning 40
  parenting 28
  patterns 29
  programs of, 13
biofeedback 52
brain 5-8
  cell growth 38
  development 28, 38
  diagram 7
  functional blocks of, 14
  functioning 3, 5-16, 27, 47
  growth spurts 30
  hemispheric 12, 41
  hemispheres 6
  integrated 16
  limbic 29, 30, 36
  lower 15
  microstructure 13
  models 3, 5, 8-16
  new 9
  organization vii
  programs 15, 35
  research 3, 5
  structures 9, 15
  transmitter chemicals 6
  waves 12
brain stem 6, 7, 9, 10, 14
Broca's area 7, 8

cell
  assemblies 14, 28
  clusters 6
  glial 13, 30
  nerve 5, 13
cerebellum 7, 9
child abuse 28
chimera 11
classroom
  application 47
  atmosphere 50, 52
  communication 36
  noise 37
cognition 5
communication 21
  adult-child 36
  evolving 21
  interdisciplinary 47
  interhemispheric 12, 30, 31, 49
  modeling 37
  verbal and nonverbal classroom 36

corpus callosum 10, 11, 12, 28, 30
cortex 6, 8, 9, 10, 14, 15
  new 9
  see also neocortex
cues 36, 37
curriculum 20, 49
dendrites 6
dendritic branching 30
development
  brain 28
  career 28, 29
  child 10
  classical themes of, 3
  cognitive 20
  curricular 49
  ego 28
  human vii, 27, 39, 47
  individuals and, 27-33
  language 25, 39, 47
  life-span 27-29
  linguistic 20
  neurological 3, 29, 30-32
  priorities 48
  stages 27
  whole-child 8
developmental lifeline 27, 28
dichaptic tests 12
dichotic technique 12
discrepancy 37
DNA genetic preprogramming 15
drawing competence 50
drugs 13, 38, 42

educator 20, 21, 24, 47, 48
electroencephalogram (EEG) 12
emotion 5, 16, 50, 51
engram 15
environment 35-43, 47
  language 23
  learning 22, 35, 41
enzymes 13
epileptics 10
ERIC Clearinghouse on Elementary
  and Early Childhood Education 48
exceptionality 39-42
expectancy vii, 35, 36, 37
  power of, 36
  programmed 35
experience 30

family therapist 28
flexibility 41
function 9, 10, 14, 20, 32
  brain 3, 5-16
  gating 6, 10

generativeness 40

hemisphere 11
  cortical 7
  left 8, 10, 11, 12, 15, 28, 30, 32, 36, 38, 49
  left and right strategies 48
  right 10, 11, 12, 14, 28, 30, 32, 36, 38, 49
hemispheric processing 11, 49
hippocampus 6, 14
homeostasis 9
hormones 6, 9, 13, 42
  limbic system 9
hypothalamus 6, 15

imagery 35, 38-39
imaging 21
individuality 40, 41
inheritance 41
instinct 9
interdisciplinary collaboration 47

knowledge 21

language vii, 15, 21, 22, 38
  conceptual aspects of, 8
  deficits 10
  development 19-25, 39
  functions 7
  learning 32
lateralization
  hemispheric 3, 50
leadership 48, 53
learning 16, 36, 38, 39, 47, 48, 50, 52
  behavior 3
  cognitive 20
  dimensions of, 5
  disabilities 42, 50
  environment 22, 41
  first- and second-language 32
  generative 5, 35, 52

materials 41
motor 31
motoric base of, 49
process vii, 3, 17-43
style 27, 28, 39-42, 50
   right-brain 30
systems view of, 5
tasks 39
lessons 20
life span 28
   development 27-29
   developmental sequence 41
limbic system 6, 9, 50
   middle 9
literacy instruction 24
lobe
   frontal 6, 8, 15, 29
   occipital 14
   parietal 14
   temporal 8, 14
localization 8
locomotion 19
logic 20

mainstreaming 42
malnutrition 38
mathematics 12
memory 15, 38
   concept-building 39
   function 51
   short-term 28
message
   environmental 37-38
metalinguistic awareness 24
midbrain 6, 8, 9
   homeostatic mechanism 10
   limbic structures of, 6
model vii, 8-16
   early childhood education 27
   generative learning vii, 35
   integrative 51
   interaction 49
   learning-styles 42
   life-span development 28
   of cognitive style 41
   of creativity 49
   performance 35
modeling 35-37

monologues
   extended child vii, 19, 21, 22, 24
motor
   action 7
   control 8, 10
   experience 30
   involvement 19
   learning 31
   meanings 19, 20
motoric meaning 21
   development of vii, 19-21, 24
muscle coordination 7
music 12
myelination 30, 38
   cycle 31

National Association for the Education
   of Young Children 48
neocortex 9, 15, 51, 52
nerves 5, 6, 13
nervous system
   central 5, 6
   human 9
neuroanatomy 8
neurochemistry 3, 13
neurological substrates 36
neurological system 9
neurology
   developmental 32
neuron 13, 14
neuronal linkages 13
neuropsychology 8
neurosurgery 8
neurotransmitters 13

olfactory bulb 6
orientation
   altruistic 30
   lateral 19
orthography 24

parenting 28
paths 6
pathways 13
   motor 6
   sensory 6
peptides 13
personality 40
phlogenetic scale 9

phrenology 8
Piaget 30
play 19, 20, 24, 32
policy 47-48
print
   early conceptions of, vii, 19, 22-25
   exploration 23, 24
processing
   cognitive 3, 12
   styles 13
professional activity vii, 47-48
program
   brain 15, 42
   early childhood 21, 22, 24
   food 38
   implications 47, 48-50
proster events 14

reading 24, 50
   conventions of, 25
   comprehension 39
registers 32
relationships
   spatial 12
Reptilian complex (R-complex) 9
research
   brain vii, 52
   interdisciplinary 3
   lingusitic 32
   neurological 5
   on malnutrition 38
response
   flight-fight 52
   survival 9
responsiveness 41
reticular activating system (RAS) 6, 9, 10, 14
   gates 10
   model 8
reticular formation 14
risk-taking 41
rules 21, 22, 32

senescence 28
sense of humor 41
sensitive period 29-30, 42
sensitivity 41
sex differences 37-38

skill
   language 49
   linear 48
   listening 21-22
   right-hemisphere 50
   verbal 50
   visuo-spatial 32
Society for Research in Child Development 48
sound
   early conceptions of, vii, 19, 22-25
speech 20-22
spelling 22-25
spinal cord 6
split brain 10, 11, 12
stream of consciousness 49
stress 52
synapse 6, 13, 14
synaptic sites 13

taking turns 21
talk 22
teaching styles 28
tempo 41
thalamus 6
theory
   brain functioning vii, 19
   developmental learning 32
   Piagetian 30
thinking 9, 30, 38
triune 9

verbal
   ability 49, 50
   aspects of language 24
   communication 36
   fluency 20, 32
visual space
   left and right 11
vocalization 19

waves
   alpha 12
   beta 12, 30
Wernicke's area 7, 8
writing 21, 22, 24, 25, 50

Selected NAEYC Publications

If this book is helpful to you—
1. NAEYC's journal *Young Children* is available through membership or by subscription. Write to NAEYC for further information.
2. Many other teaching ideas are included in the books listed below. Order your copies today.
3. Order ten or more copies each of this or other NAEYC books as texts for classes or workshops and receive a ten percent discount.

Code #	Title	Price
315	Administration: Making Programs Work for Children and Families	$5.50
106	Art: Basic for Young Children	$4.95
318	The American Family: Myths and Reality	$2.20
132	The Block Book	$3.85
200	Careers with Young Children: Making Your Decision	$4.40
213	Caring: Supporting Children's Growth	$2.20
127	Cognitively Oriented Curriculum	$4.95
402S	Cómo Reconocer un Buen Programa de Educación Pre-Escolar	$ .30
313	Cultural Awareness: A Resource Bibliography	$5.20
104	Current Issues in Child Development	$3.85
121	Developmental Screening in Early Childhood: A Guide	$2.75
314	Directory of Educational Programs for Adults Who Work with Children	$3.30
112	Ethical Behavior in Early Childhood Education	$2.00
212	A Good Beginning for Babies: Guidelines for Group Care	$5.75
317	GROUP Games in Early Education: Implications of Piaget's Theory	$9.35
302	A Guide to Discipline	$1.65
105	Ideas That Work with Young Children, Vol. 2	$4.75
130	Imagination: Key to Human Potential	$3.85
316	More than Graham Crackers: Nutrition Education and Food Preparation with Young Children	$4.20
312	Mother/Child, Father/Child Relationships	$5.20
107	Music in Our Lives: The Early Years	$2.75
135	Parent Involvement in Early Childhood Education	$3.30
208	Perspectives on Child Care	$1.40
102	Piaget, Children, and Number	$2.20

115	Planning Environments for Young Children: Physical Space	$2.00
306	Play as a Learning Medium	$3.00
126	Promoting Cognitive Growth	$3.00
309	Science with Young Children	$3.55
128	The Significance of the Young Child's Motor Development	$2.45
402E	Some Ways of Distinguishing a Good Early Childhood Program	$ .30
310	Talks with Teachers: Reflections on Early Childhood Education	$3.30
305	Teacher Education	$2.50
311	Teaching Practices: Reexamining Assumptions	$2.50

Order from NAEYC
        1834 Connecticut Avenue, N.W.
        Washington, DC 20009

All prices include postage and handling. Please enclose full payment for orders under $10.

For information about these and other NAEYC publications, write for a free publications brochure.